The Blandford Book of
Traditional Handicrafts

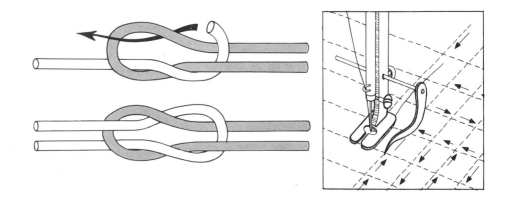

The Blandford Book of
Traditional Handicrafts

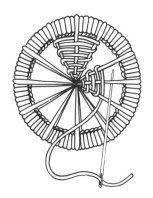
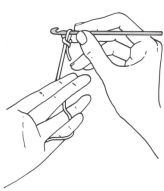

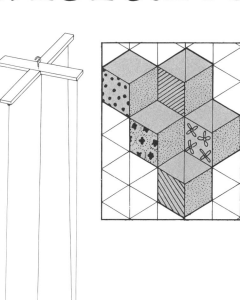

EDITED BY

John Rome

BLANDFORD PRESS
POOLE   DORSET

First published in the U.K. 1981

Copyright © 1981 Blandford Press Ltd,
Link House, West Street,
Poole, Dorset, BH15 1LL

British Library Cataloguing in Publication Data

The Blandford book of traditional handicrafts.
1 Handicraft
I. Rome, John
745.5   TT155

ISBN 0 7137 0951 0

Designed by Oxprint Ltd
Illustrations by Oxford Illustrators Ltd

Phototypeset by Oliver Burridge & Co. Ltd, Crawley

Printed in Great Britain by Hazell Watson & Viney Ltd, Aylesbury

Contents

Foreword

Perhaps one of the most difficult and frustrating things to do is to edit a book on subjects of which one has only a limited knowledge. In my case this was very true, but, knowing most of the contributors personally, my task was made easier by their patience, good humour and long suffering through endless sessions of questioning and being shown 'how to do it'. With their encouragement, all the problems were eventually overcome and this book compiled.

Nearly all crafts today rely on traditional skills although, in many instances, the materials are more interesting and the colours wider-ranging.

Some of the traditional crafts, such as smocking, are now coming back into fashion. The making of Dorset buttons, once a thriving industry, largely ceased with the advent of machines, but now, happily, a few people are again making these delicate fastenings. Hand-made lace is another art that is being revived and kept alive by enthusiastic teachers.

While editing this book I was very surprised by some of the things which I discovered. The candlemaker, for instance, no longer uses tallow now that paraffin wax, which is clean and easy to handle, is available. Quick-drying adhesives have taken the place of the rather messy old glues. Then there are gold and silver threads that don't tarnish, a vast range of modern materials, both natural and synthetic, and an enormous choice of colour. And yet one can still find beautiful old ivory and bone bobbins colourfully beaded—an old craft in themselves.

I was impressed by the ingenuity of the puppet-maker and her use of a plastic flowerpot, the artistry of the pressed flower designs, the intricacies of the needlecraft and the many and varied uses to which a simple knot can be put. You will discover many exciting things to make as you thumb through these chapters on traditional crafts—either for the home or as gifts. The techniques are carefully described and illustrated with both diagrams and colour plates. It is sincerely hoped that you, the reader, will gain a great deal of pleasure in filling your leisure hours creatively.

In conclusion, I would like to thank all those who so kindly lent articles for the colour plates and, most particularly, the contributors, for it is their knowledge which has made this book so interesting and informative.

John Rome

SEAN LUDGATE

Ropecraft, Macramé and Netting

THE ART of knot-making dates back to primitive man who found ways to tie simple knots in cords made from animal skins, vegetable fibres and strips of bark. Over the centuries, knots were developed to suit the needs of many different trades; the farmer, the weaver, the miller, the fisherman and many others, all contributed their special designs. However, undoubtedly the greatest advance in knot-making was made, prior to the era of the clipper ships in the mid-nineteenth century, by sailors who spread the art of knot-making to every part of the world.

Before the end of the eighteenth century, rope was made entirely by hand. This required the chosen material to be worked in a series of twists, each twist going in the opposite direction to the previous twist in order to make the rope hard and tight. With the advent of machinery, by the middle of the nineteenth century, smaller cordage, such as string and twine, was manufactured.

Many miles of rope and cordage were used aboard ship; apart from standing- and running-rigging, rope was needed for the attachment, protection or decoration of equipment such as stanchions, tillers, gangways, spars and decks; thus there was always an ample supply of raw materials available. Few sailors were able to read or write, so the manual pastimes, such as ropecraft or scrimshaw (bone-carving), offered a release from the hours of boredom off watch. There was a lively rivalry in producing new and individual designs and much exchange of ideas with sailors and other craftsmen in foreign ports.

Two types of knotting evolved, the practical used aboard ship, such as ladder-mats, thump-mats, coach-whipping, fenders, bell-ropes, and Turk's-heads, and the purely decorative knotting made in thin twines, known as 'McNamara's Lace' or macramé. The word 'macramé' is believed to have been derived from the Arabic *miqramah*, meaning a 'veil' or 'shawl' which was decorated with a knotted fringe. This type of knotting has been found in many parts of the world; samples dating back over six hundred years have been found in places as far apart as Egypt, South America and China. Thus, knotting was an international art. However, although practical knots have been in regular use by sailors and other trades, decorative knotting became almost a lost art until recent years when ropecraft and macramé were revived in Great Britain, helped considerably by the exotic designs imported from the USA and Canada.

The wide range of cordage made from many different materials provides great scope for knot-making. Although at first glance some designs may appear complicated, in fact, the beginner will be agreeably surprised to find that pleasing results can be achieved without prior knowledge or practice.

There are, of course, more advanced designs which cannot be made merely by following a pattern. Like any artist, it is necessary to develop that indefinable sense for the shape and feel of the knot as it takes form through many stages. Such work needs a great deal of practice.

Materials and equipment

soft board or cork, marked out in
   2.5 cm (1 in) squares
pins
darning needles
yarns, cords, twine, string or rope
   of different types and thicknesses
tape measure
scissors

rubber bands
pencil
glue
wooden beads
12.5 cm (5 in) gauge or spacer
netting needle
netting twine

CHOICE OF MATERIALS

For the beginner, choosing a suitable type and size of material from the great variety of cordage available may present a bewildering problem. Price, of course, is one important factor. However, the cheapest may, in the end, prove a disappointment, leading to the abandonment of further effort, instead of fascination and pleasure, so a few words on the construction and properties of the most popular materials may be helpful.

Almost any material can be used for knotting: leather, animal skin and plastic thonging, animal wool yarn, natural vegetable fibre or synthetic yarn cords. However, the appearance and detail of the knot-work will be governed by the construction and the yarn tension. Apart from single strand materials, such as plastic or animal thonging, there are two main constructions: twisted and braided (plaited). In twisted construction, the individual fibres are twisted into yarns, which are in turn twisted back in the opposite direction to form strands. This twisting greatly increases the strength of the rope. A slack twist produces a soft pliable cord, which is easy to work, but tends to unlay and flatten when knotted, causing the knots to blend together and lose their distinctive pattern. Because the yarns in braided cord are closely interlocked in the criss-cross pattern of the plait, the shape of the knot is more apparent.

In the choice of cord much depends upon the type of work involved; a soft yarn with slack tension is attractive when used for pot-hangers, wall-hangings and room-dividers, where the natural 'shaggy' look is required, but for intricate knot-work, belts, bottle-coverings, mats and individual decorative knots, the ideal is a cord with a medium tension, which will not flatten easily, but is still sufficiently pliable to work.

Pre-stretched and tightly braided cords, such as sash-cord, are hard on the hands, stiff to work and are not recommended.

Ropes and cords made from both natural and synthetic yarns have advantages and disadvantages, depending upon the type of article to be made and the required finish. For a natural effect, jute, sisal, hemp, flax and cotton are all suitable. Jute is the least expensive, but soft jute twine tends to shed its fibres when being worked, which can be a nuisance. Sisal is another rather hairy material which sheds fibres and is less pliable than jute; it is also rather prickly on the hands. Hemp, flax and cotton are excellent, cotton being particularly good for making intricate knotting.

Cotton twines are supplied in numbered sizes which can be a bit confusing; you may find the following guide useful:

Size 1 is approximately 3.5 mm (7/50 in) diameter
Size 2 is approximately 3.0 mm (6/50 in) diameter
Size 3 is approximately 2.5 mm (5/50 in) diameter
Size 4 is approximately 2.0 mm (4/50 in) diameter
Size 5 is approximately 1.5 mm (3/50 in) diameter
Size 7 is approximately 0.5 mm (1/50 in) diameter

Most braided cords and three-strand ropes are measured by diameter in millimetres, but jute and sisal twines are often supplied by weight and mention is made of the number of plies used in its construction; this latter is no guide to the thickness as you can obtain a four-ply which is as thick as eight-ply so you must resort to consulting the pattern, which usually gives a full size inset illustration of the thickness to be used.

The majority of natural fibre cords have good gripping properties and they can be obtained in a range of attractive colours; however, the colours in some twines tend to fade when exposed to strong sunlight and, unless specially treated, the twines will deteriorate in damp conditions.

Synthetic twines, such as rayon, nylon, terylene, acrylic, polypropylene, are not so susceptible to fading and will not deteriorate if used outdoors for such items as garden plant-hangers, nets and hammocks. Most will work well and a matt finish is preferable to a gloss, which tends to be more slippery. The worst offenders in this respect are mono-filament threads and polythene twisted line as used for fishing; the latter has a particularly slippery texture. Another advantage of synthetics is that they can be melted with a hot iron, which is most convenient for sealing the ends, or fusing ends to the adjoining strands in articles such as bracelets and scarf-rings, thus saving the bother of whipping or resorting to the use of adhesives.

Three-strand ropes, however, must be cut with a hot knife to preserve the twist tension, otherwise the strands will immediately unlay themselves and become limp and shapeless. When forming individual three-strand knots in synthetic material, each strand must be heat-sealed and you must constantly try to maintain the twist in the strands while making the knot, or they will flatten and spoil the distinctive pattern.

Ropecraft

SIMPLE KNOTS

There are many hundreds of knots for securing, joining, terminating or forming loops in rope, but we are dealing here with only a few of those in common use. Knowing how to tie knots efficiently saves time and trouble, to say nothing of the lives that depend on correct and secure knots. The sailor up in the rigging, the climber and cowboy, and many others, owe their safety to the well-tied knot.

Below
Figure 1.1

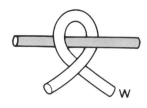

Half-hitch This is the simplest form of knot and forms the foundation of the clove-hitch. Although incomplete by itself, it forms the basis for other knots and, when used in series, will form a pattern, such as in rib-hitching and macramé designs, and give additional security when finishing off other knots.

To tie a half-hitch, the working end 'W' is taken round the fixed cord and behind the standing part (Fig. 1.1). A series of half-hitches is illustrated in Fig. 1.2.

Left to right
Figures 1.2–4

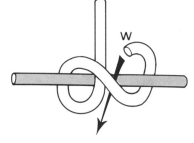
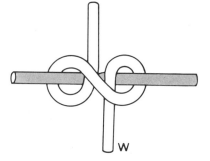

Below
Figure 1.5

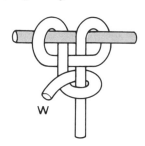

Clove-hitch Two half-hitches form a clove-hitch, best known of all hitches, a valuable knot which holds well the harder the pull against it and is not prone to jam (Fig. 1.3 & 4). The addition of a further half-hitch round the standing part will give added security (Fig. 1.5).

Reef-knot How often must the owner of a boat regret that he did not learn to tie the simple and effective reef-knot! The average person is often ill-informed on the subject and, even securing a parcel with string, or tying his shoe-laces, ends up with a granny-knot (Fig. 1.6 & 7). This is, in fact, a reef-knot crossed the wrong way. The reef-knot differs from the granny in that the working end is passed behind both standing parts of the loop (Fig. 1.8 & 9). It is a better way of joining two lengths of rope. Originally used for joining reef points (cords) fitted through a sail, and used to gather up, or reef, the sail in rough weather, it can be undone easily, even when it has been under load, unlike the granny-knot which jams solid and has to be attacked with a sharp instrument if it is ever to be undone! The reef (Fig. 1.10) forms the basis of macramé square-knotting.

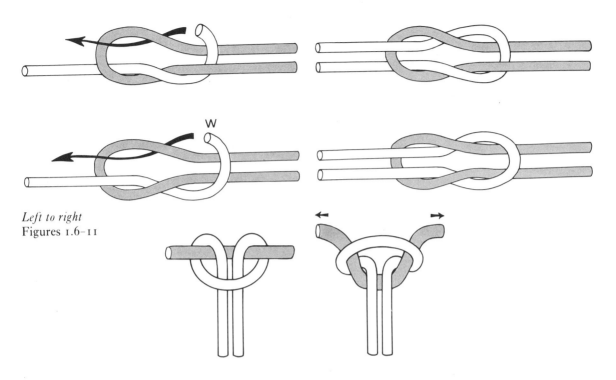

Left to right
Figures 1.6–11

Cow-hitch The reef-knot is liable to capsize if used to join two cords of different sizes. In the situation where the tail end and standing part of the thicker rope can be pulled in opposite directions (Fig. 1.11), the result will be to form a cow-hitch or lark's-head, which will allow the thicker cord to slip through the loops of the smaller.

BENDS

Knots for joining two ropes together are called bends.

Below
Figures 1.12–13

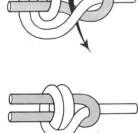

Sheet-bend A quick and reliable way of joining a smaller rope to a larger one, is by using a sheet-bend, single or double, the latter being more secure.

Make a loop in the larger rope and pass the end of the smaller rope through the loop. Take the working end and pass it behind both parts of the standing part of the larger rope, take it over the loop twice and under the standing part of the smaller rope and pull tight (Fig. 1.12 & 13).

Carrick bend This is another bend in common use. Form a loop in the middle of one rope, cross end 'B' over end 'A'. Place the working end of the joining rope behind the loop, take the working end and pass it over the upper crossed parts of 'A' and 'B', down between the cross-overs (Fig. 1.14), then over the standing loop, under the working end and over the standing loop, and pull tight (Fig. 1.15 & 16).

The same configuration, but with cross-overs in the opposite direction, forms the Josephine knot, which is used in decorative knotting (see Fig. 1.85 & 86).

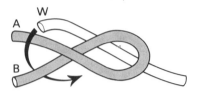  

Left to right
Figures 1.14–16

TERMINAL KNOTS

Two knots, each with a different purpose, are illustrated.

Blood-knot This was originally used on the tails of the notorious cat-o'nine-tails and is one of the most simple and effective terminal knots. It can be used to stop a cord slipping through an eyelet or as a decoration on lanyards or door-screen cords instead of wooden beads.

To make this knot, take the standing end in the left hand and pass the working end of the rope over the standing end twice (Fig. 1.17) and pull both ends tight (Fig. 1.18).

Below
Figures 1.17 & 18

Monkey's-fist This is a more elaborate knot designed to contain a weight, such as a lead-shot. The weight in the knot on the end of a light line enabled the line to be thrown considerable distances from the jetty to the vessel which was coming alongside. Once on board, the line, called a heaving-line, was used as a messenger to haul ashore the heavy mooring cables. The monkey's-fist, made in coloured braid-line with a marble in the centre, makes an attractive pendant.

To make the monkey's-fist, pass three loops round the fingers—not too tightly—(Fig. 1.19). Pass the working end three times round the first three loops (Fig. 1.20). Remove the knot from the fingers and pass the working end through the spaces which were occupied by the index and second fingers (Fig. 1.21 & 22). At this point, insert the marble or lead-shot and tighten up the loops (Fig. 1.23). The working end can now be cut off and, if of synthetic cord, it can be fused to secure the knot.

Left to right
Figures 1.19 & 20

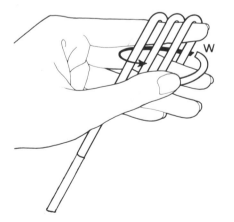 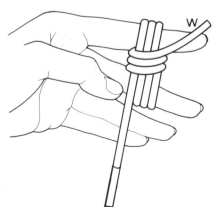

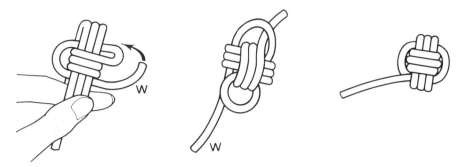

Left to right
Figures 1.21-23

DECORATIVE KNOTS

When forming a decorative knot it is important to visualise the finished appearance; avoid over-tightening the loops in the early stages. Once the shape has been produced in a single strand form, follow round, tightening each loop in turn and taking care to preserve the shape at all times until the knot is complete.

Turk's-head One of the most versatile of the decorative knots is the Turk's-head. Used aboard sailing ships to decorate tillers, stanchions, man-ropes and other nautical equipment, it can be made in the form of a ring to encircle an object or woven as a flat knot to make mats. When making the knot in a ring form, it is similar to a circular plait, the diameter being governed by the number of tucks; two, five, seven or more may be used. The width can be varied by the number of times the working end is passed round the pattern.

Wide Turk's-heads can be made using several parts, but these are for the more advanced knot-maker, so the single part knot, which can be learned with a few minutes practice, is described.

Take a good length of cord in the left hand, 3 mm ($\frac{1}{8}$ in) diameter is a suitable size for practice. Make a loop round the fingers (Fig. 1.24) at 'A', cross the working end to the left and trap it under the thumb. Pass the working end behind the fingers again to form loop 'B', cross over the end of loop 'A' and trap the cross-overs of both loops under the thumb. Check that both loops are equal in size and larger than the final diameter required (Fig. 1.25).

Turn the fingers horizontally, tuck the working end under loop 'A' and over loop 'B' to the left (Fig. 1.26). Cross loop 'B' over loop 'A' and tuck the working end under 'A' and over 'B' to the right (Fig. 1.27).

Left to right
Figures 1.24-27

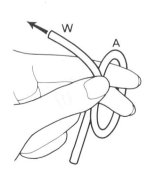
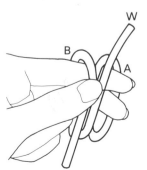
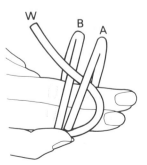
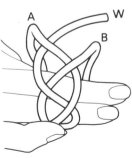

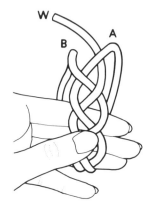

Release your grip on the first cross-over; rotate the knot in your fingers and grip the second cross-over. Cross loop 'B' to the left over 'A', pass the working end under 'A' and over 'B', to the left (Fig. 1.28). Repeat this procedure twice more and the working end can be passed into the knot alongside the tail end (Fig. 1.29).

Keeping to the right-hand side, and parallel to the tail cord, weave the working end round the knot two or three times as required (Fig. 1.30). The knot is now ready for mounting, on a jig for tightening, or directly onto the object to be decorated. If it is to be used in flat form, complete the knot in single strand form to Fig. 1.29, then place the knot on a flat surface and weave as illustrated in Fig. 1.31.

Examples of simple domestic objects and decorations using the Turk's-head are: scarf-rings, bracelets, table-napkin rings, table-mats, pot-stands and decoration on pots, jars and bottles.

As it is often necessary to produce Turk's-heads to a uniform diameter, a jig or former is used. In the case of the scarf-ring, for example, this can be a simple wooden dowel around which the loops are tightened as in Fig. 1.32. When complete, the ends are cut with a small soldering iron, such as is used for radio repairs; this fuses them permanently (Fig. 1.33).

The jig for a bracelet can be made from plastic tubing (Fig. 1.34), the ends being fused inside the bracelet (Fig. 1.35). For making mats, the jig has a raised centre portion with a number of sides appropriate to the number of tucks used (Fig. 1.36). This ensures that the form of the Turk's-head is made regular. When finished, a Flemish coil is placed in the centre and both Turk's-head and coil are glued onto felt or some other rigid material (Fig. 1.37).

Flemish coil Although it cannot be described as a knot, this provides a useful method of covering flat or curved surfaces. It is easier to form the coil on a flat piece of cardboard so that it may be moved about. If the coil is to be fitted into the middle of a Turk's-head, a circle or parallel lines of the correct width can be drawn on the cardboard.

To make the Flemish coil, first make sure you have a length of cord long enough to make up the coil to the desired size. Double back one end of the cord about 0.5 mm ($\frac{1}{4}$ in) to form the start. Place the end flat on the cardboard and, with finger and thumb, turn in the direction required, feeding the cord at a

Above
Figures 1.28–31
Left to right
Figures 1.32 & 33

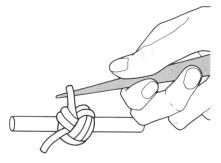

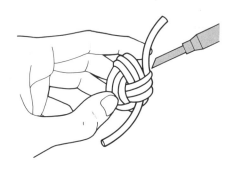

Left to right
Figures 1.34–37

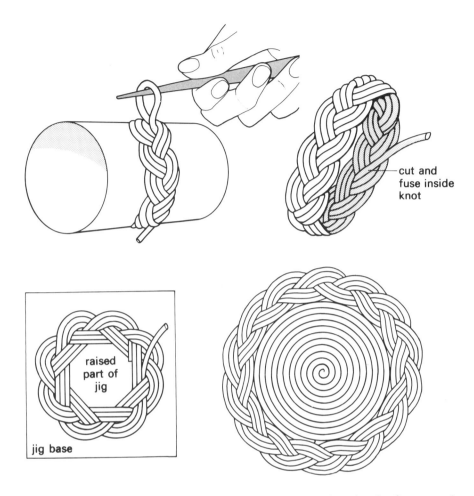

cut and
fuse inside
knot

raised
part of
jig

jig base

light even tension while keeping the coil flat on the card under the fingers and palm of the hand. When the correct size is reached, insert a pin through the outer turns to secure (Fig. 1.38 & 39).

Fig. 1.40 shows an example of a Turk's-head being used to decorate a plastic flower-pot which has been covered with cord. If the Turk's-head is made in a contrasting colour, the effect is very attractive.

Left to right
Figures 1.38–40

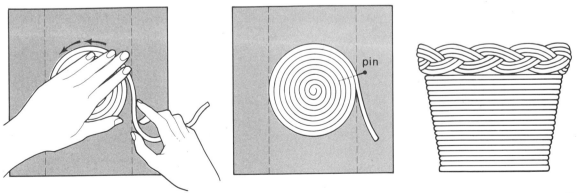

pin

FLAT KNOTS

Two of the better known flat knots are the prolong-knot and the thump-mat. Both had their practical uses aboard ship, the prolong-knot being used to provide grip on gangway treads and as deck-mats. The thump-mat was fitted over the ring-bolts which secured blocks to the deck, in order to protect the deck from chafe. Both these knots can be used to make attractive mats for domestic use.

Prolong-knot Again make absolutely certain that you start with enough cord to finish the job, as it can be most frustrating to find you only need a few inches to complete your mat! Start by making the first three stages of a four-loop Turk's-head, starting in the middle of a length of cord so that the tail and working ends are equal, as follows:

Below
Figures 1.41–45

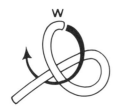

With the standing end at your left pass the working end across it to form a loop, bring the working end back and pass it over the loop and under the standing end (Fig. 1.41).

Weave the working end through the top loop, under the standing end, over the loop and under the right hand loop (Fig. 1.42). You will now be at the stage illustrated in Fig. 1.43. (Fig. 1.44 & 45 show the next and final stages of the four-loop Turk's-head as a matter of interest.)

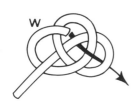

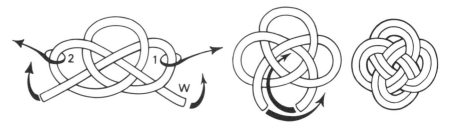

Having arrived at this stage, place the knot on a flat surface and pull out loops 1 and 2 (Fig. 1.46). Take the left loop 2 and twist it to the right (Fig. 1.47). Now take the right-hand loop 1 and twist it to the right, then place it across loop 2 (Fig. 1.48). Weave the left-hand end of the cord 'A' under loop 2, over both parts of loop 1, and under loop 2 (Fig. 1.49). Now weave the end of cord 'B' over 1, under 2, over 'A', under 2 and over 1 (Fig. 1.49). Care must be taken to preserve the position of the loops at all times. The ends emerge under and over their respective loops and are then passed back into the knot to follow round the pattern two or three times as necessary (Fig. 1.50).

Thump-mat Like the prolong-knot, the positions of the loops must be maintained at all times at each stage.

Take a good length of cord, enough for the size of mat you wish to make. Start with a double cross-over (Fig. 1.51). Take the working end 'A' across, over itself, and pass it through the top of the initial loop (Fig. 1.52). End 'B' is then passed under the bottom of loop 'A', under the initial loop, over 'A' under 'B' and out over the loop formed by 'A' on the left-hand side (Fig. 1.53). End

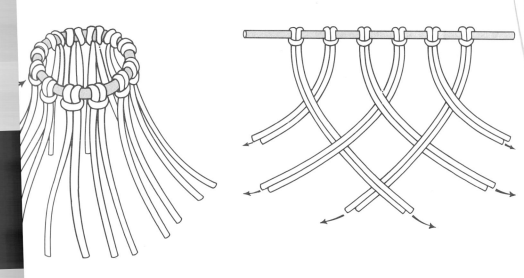

right
s 1.56

s 1.58

be linked together to form a continuous covering, such as the half-hitch, clove-hitch, sennets, coach-whipping, square-knots, Carrick bends and Josephine knots, to mention a few.

Coach-whipping This is a type of sennet, or plait. Start by making a ring—if synthetic cord is used, solder the ends—with enough cord to fit over the neck of a bottle, bearing in mind that the ring would need to accommodate a number of hitches before placing it over the neck. Take fourteen long cords, each 1.5 m (5 ft) long and 3 mm ($\frac{1}{8}$ in) in diameter; hitch these at their mid-length to the ring and fit over the neck of the bottle (Fig. 1.56). The inset shows the cow-hitch, which is made by forming a loop in the middle of the cord which is then passed behind the rope ring, the two ends being brought over the front of the ring and slipped through the loop.

The strands can now be woven in pairs, in sequence as illustrated in Fig. 1.57. After completing the first two or three sets of cross-overs, it will be necessary to tighten them. Slip a rubber band over the neck of the bottle to hold them in position while you work downwards. When the work reaches the widest part of the bottle, the cross-overs must spread out (Fig. 1.58), which makes the work a bit more difficult. However, by securing with another band and tightening each set of cross-overs, the pattern can be adjusted to form a symmetrical design. When the bottom of the bottle is reached, glue all the ends to the bottle and, when the glue is set, cut off the excess cord ends.

A Turk's-head, using about 5.5 m (6 yd) of cord, fitted round the base will hide the endings and make a neat finish. For added decoration, a Turk's-head may also be fitted round the neck at the top and base (Fig. 1.59).

Spiral-hitching Using a long length of cord, about 5.5 m (6 yd), make a loop in one end, 'B', making sure that, when tied, the loop will be large enough to fit over the neck of a bottle after being hitched. Pass end 'B' through the loop and round the standing parts of the loop, cross over 'A', under 'B', and out between the loop. Pull the ends tight and cut end 'B' short (Fig. 1.60 & inset). This, of

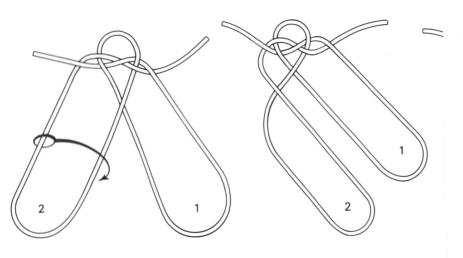

cow
hitch

Left to right
Figures 1.46–50

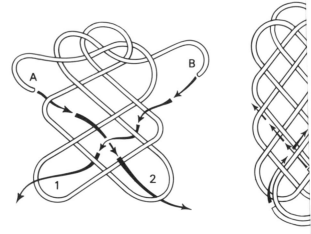

Below
Figures 1.51–55

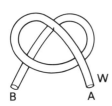

'B' is now passed under, over, under and over both
passed over, under, over and under (Fig. 1.54). You
left and end 'B' to the right-hand side of the knot as
Follow the pattern round, weaving both ends in the
under and over, until you have a closely woven mat.

COVERING A BOTTLE

Another useful function for ropecraft is the covering
their protection as well as decoration. There are many

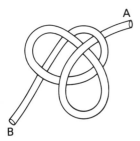

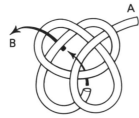

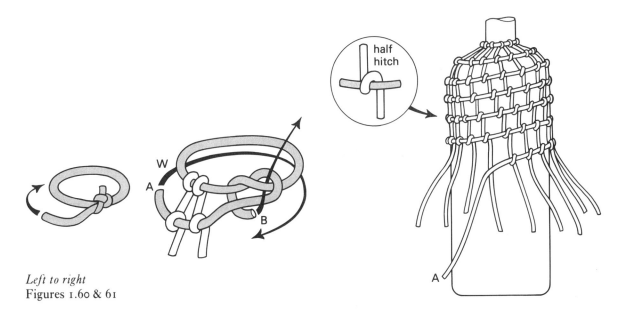

Left to right
Figures 1.60 & 61

course, would be for the knot used with natural fibre; if using synthetic cord then heat-fuse the end to itself.

Take a number of long cords, remembering each one should be about five times the length of the bottle, loop each one by means of a half-hitch (see inset) at their mid-lengths onto the ring and fit them over the neck of the bottle.

Make one round turn round the neck of the bottle with the long end 'A' and half-hitch each of the working ends in turn round the long cord. Continue winding the long cord round the bottle, making rows of half-hitches at each turn (Fig. 1.61). If necessary the hitches can be made more closely than illustrated. This type of hitching can also be used in a flat form and is often seen in macramé designs for belts and bags.

Rib-hitching This type of covering can be made more easily by using a packing needle or, better still, a Swedish marline spike, for passing the working end behind the hitches.

To begin, make two turns of the cord, again using a good length, round the bottle and secure with a cow-hitch (see Fig. 1.56 & inset). Continue round the initial two turns of the cord, making a series of cow-hitches (Fig. 1.62). When the circle is completed, pass the working end in a clockwise direction behind the first cow-hitch, pull tight, and do likewise round each of the cow-hitches in turn (Fig. 1.63). As you continue the rib effect will take shape (Fig. 1.64).

MAN-ROPE OR TACK-KNOT

Although this was originally tied at the end of a three-stranded sheet attached to the clew of a square sail, the man-rope knot is also used in man-ropes to provide handgrips on gangways. Similar ropes are sometimes used down the sides of domestic stairways, so this useful knot should not be omitted here. Apart from the need to secure the rope at each end, to prevent it pulling through

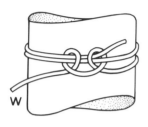 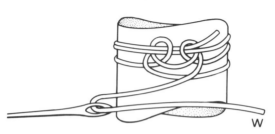 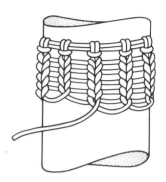

Left to right
Figures 1.62–64

the supporting rings, a man-rope knot will look much more professional than a round turn and lashing.

The man-rope knot is formed in two stages. First take a three-stranded rope about 20mm (in) in diameter, unlay the strands for about 30cm (12in), place a whipping round the rope, to prevent the strands from unlaying further, and whip or tape the ends of each strand to prevent the yarns from fraying out. Holding the rope vertically in the hand, make one horizontal loop in strand 1 in an anticlockwise direction (Fig. 1.65). Pass strand 2 over 1 and under strands 1 and 3 (Fig. 1.66). Pass strand 3 under the tail end of 2 and up through the original loop (Fig. 1.67). Pull in the slack ends to make an even pattern, but not too tightly. This first stage is called a wall-knot and it can, if required, be followed round a second time to make a decorative knot on its own, which will have the ends coming out of the top.

Below
Figures 1.65–69

To complete the man-rope knot, you now make a crown-sennet on top (Fig. 1.80–2). At this stage the knot should look like Fig. 1.68. Follow round the wall-knots and crown-sennets a second and, if wished, a third time, and finish by tucking the ends down the centre. A marline spike will facilitate this operation. Cut off the tail ends and whip under the knot if necessary. The completed knot should look like Fig. 1.69.

Fig. 1.70 illustrates a typical seachest becket, which may be converted into a handsome door knocker by the insertion of a small metal stud behind the bottom of the loop, using crown-sennets and Turk's-head knots. Fig. 1.71 illustrates a design for a ship's bell lanyard, which could be adapted for domestic use using the same knots as in Fig. 1.70.

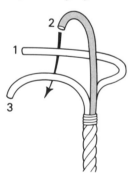

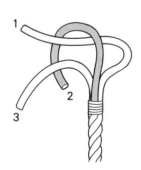  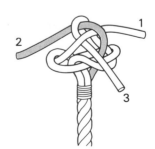 

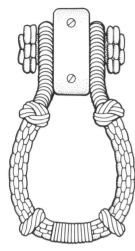

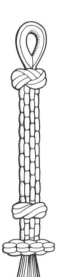

Macramé

Study the section on 'Ropecraft' so that you can learn to tie the basic knots used in macramé, they are the square-knot and clove-hitch. Once you have mastered them you will be able to make such things as wall-hangings, room-dividers, lampshades and many more articles. In this craft let your imagination work using interesting designs and patterns.

You must, however, choose the string, yarn, ropes or cords carefully, so that you have the appropriate material with which to make your article. Naturally, wall-hangings would require a thick yarn, while table-mats and shopping-bags, for instance, would be better in a medium one. You would use fine yarns for making trimmings for clothes or fringes on lampshades and upholstery.

Having decided on what you are going to make, you should have your tools and correct yarns ready to hand, but do make sure that your lengths of yarns are long enough to complete your work and make your colour schemes interesting by using contrasting colours and shades.

BASIC KNOTS

Square-knot This is simply a reef-knot tied round one or more 'filler' cords. If you can tie your shoe-laces you will have no difficulty in making many attractive items without any previous practice.

Start by fixing two pairs of cords, using a cow-hitch, to a ring or stick Fig. 1.72. Pass cord 'A' in front of the centre or 'filler' cords and behind 'B' (Fig. 1.73). Pass cord 'B' behind centre cords and forward through the loop formed by 'A' (Fig. 1.74). Tighten the knots as you go. Repeat this half-knot and you will produce the spiral effect (Fig. 1.75).

To complete the knot, pass 'A' back to the left in front of the cords and pass 'B' behind the 'filler' cords to come out through the loop formed by 'A' (Fig. 1.76). Repeat the complete knot and the result will be a chain of square-knots as illustrated in Fig. 1.77.

Simple square-knotting can be used for the cords to support hanging pots or baskets, shelves, and tables and for belts, leads and a host of other useful items.

It is sometimes necessary to link chains of square-knotting to make a net or

Above
Figures 1.70 & 71
Left to right
Figures 1.72–74

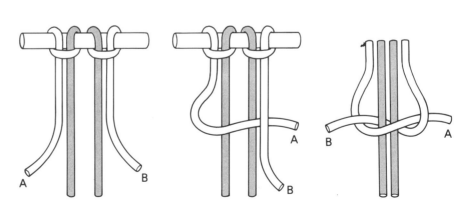

Left to right
Figures 1.75–79

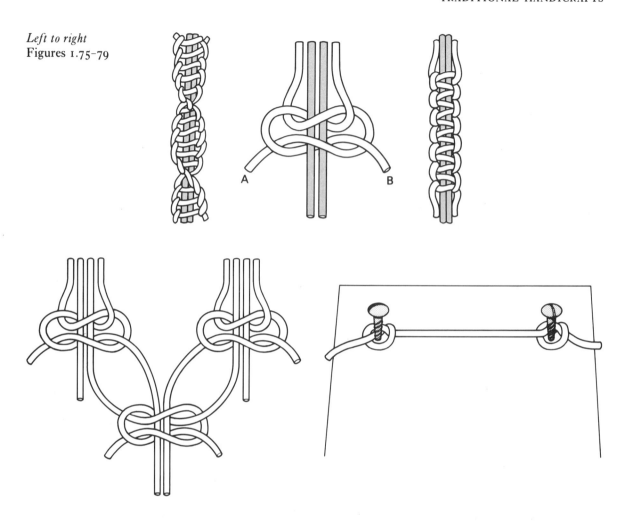

wall-hanging and you can do this by using the left and right hand working cords from two adjacent knot chains to form the 'filler' cords for an intermediate chain. The left and right hand 'filler' cords from each side chain are used as working cords (Fig. 1.78). For this you will need to mark your board at the top into 2.5 cm (1 in) squares, or you can buy a ready-marked macramé board, pin a holding line or foundation cord horizontally and fix (Fig. 1.79).

Using eight or more cords, hitch them to the holding line by means of the square-knot, making sure they are of equal length and taut. You will now have sixteen lengths hanging from the horizontal cord; now proceed tying from the instructions for the basic knot. When you have done this, link the chains of square-knotting as described above, thus making a decorative room-divider, a belt or a bag (see Fig. 1.97).

Crown-sennet This may be made from any number of cords whipped together and held vertically in the hand.

To work the knot take the required number of cords whipped together, in this case four.

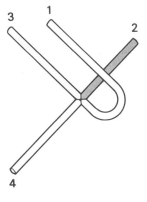

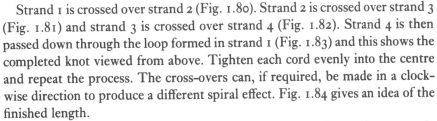

Strand 1 is crossed over strand 2 (Fig. 1.80). Strand 2 is crossed over strand 3 (Fig. 1.81) and strand 3 is crossed over strand 4 (Fig. 1.82). Strand 4 is then passed down through the loop formed in strand 1 (Fig. 1.83) and this shows the completed knot viewed from above. Tighten each cord evenly into the centre and repeat the process. The cross-overs can, if required, be made in a clockwise direction to produce a different spiral effect. Fig. 1.84 gives an idea of the finished length.

This useful type of continuous knotting can be used for making not only dog-leads, whips and lanyards, but also for covering handles or incorporating into pot-hanger designs.

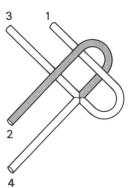

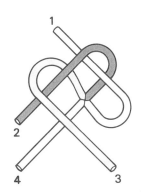

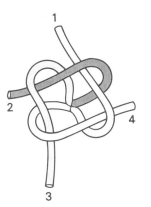

Above
Figures 1.80–84
Below
Figures 1.85 & 86

Josephine-knot This is similar to the Carrick bend and is another useful and decorative knot to incorporate in macramé designs.

Take two parallel cords, make one round turn in 'A', pass end 'B' over the loop and under and over the two ends of 'A' at either side of the cross-over (Fig. 1.85). Complete the knot by passing the working end of 'B' under the loop and crossing it over itself to emerge under the loop of 'A' (Fig. 1.86).

Whipping This is a means of binding several cords together. Take a length of 'wrapping' cord and lay one end along the cords to be bound; holding it in place with your thumb wind the loose part of the wrapping cord tightly around both the end and the cords for the required distance. To finish off, lay the other end of the wrapping cord back along the cords, take a few more tight turns and pull the end through. Trim both ends.

PLANT-POT HANGER

Very attractive plant-pot hangers may be made using any of the various yarns, twines or ropes obtainable which come in an assortment of colours and thicknesses. Use your imagination in choosing the colour and selecting the types of beads to go with the design.

For a holder approximately 0.9m (1yd) in length you will need 33.6m (36¾yd) of yarn, eight large wooden beads, and a pair of scissors.

Begin by cutting the yarn as follows: four lengths of 4.75m (5yd 6in)—A;

Figure 1.87

four lengths of 2.9 m (3 yd 6 in)—B; two lengths of 0.75 m (24 in)—these are the wrapping cords; and two lengths of 0.9 m (1 yd)—C.

Find the centre point of cords 'A' & 'B' and hold them together. Using the two 'C' cords as working cords and cords 'A' & 'B' as fillers, work a line of square knots for 16.5 cm (6½ in), i.e. 8.25 cm (3¼ in) each side of the centre. Fold the work in half and, using a wrapping cord, work 3.75 cm (1½ in) of whipping over all the cords.

Divide the cords into four groups of four—each group should have two 'A' and two 'B' cords and the two 'B' cords (short ones) should be placed in the middle of the setting.

*Work 7.6 cm (3 in) of half square knots then a further 7.5 cm (3 in) of complete square knots. Pass the two middle cords ('B') through a bead. Work one complete square knot, then pass the two middle cords ('B') through a second bead. Work a further 6.5 cm (2½ in) of complete square knots and 7.5 cm (3 in) of half square knots. Repeat from * on each group of four.

Leave 7.5 cm (3 in) of unknotted cord and, using alternate cords, work two square knots. Leave 10 cm (4 in) of unknotted cord, gather all the cords together and work 5 cm (2 in) of whipping over all the cords, using the remaining wrapping cord. Cut the cords to the required length to form a hanging fringe.

A simple pot-hanger is illustrated in Fig. 1.87.

Netting

Apart from its conventional use for fishing, netting has many domestic uses: screens for the protection of, or against, animals and small children, garden nets, safety nets, hammocks, nets for all ball games, and nets for storing and carrying.

BASIC TECHNIQUE

You will need netting needles (Fig. 1.88) of different sizes, on which to wind the twine, and a piece of wood called a gauge or spacer, approximately 12.5 cm (5 in) long. The latter is roughly elliptical in shape; its circumference equals the length of one half of the diamond pattern. For fishing nets, this gauge must conform to the appropriate mesh size set down by fishing regulations, but for domestic use you can fashion a piece of wood to suit your own requirements (Fig. 1.89). Different sizes are available from yacht chandlers to suit the size of twine to be used.

To make a net first tie a cord tightly between two fixed points. The length of the cord governs the width of net. Using the gauge as a guide to mesh size, make a series of clove-hitches along the fixed line at equal spaces, creating a series of loops of half mesh height (Fig. 1.90).

The first row of full mesh will be worked from right to left, the first loop being full mesh height (Fig. 1.91). Pass the needle behind the back of the gauge and forward through the first loop. Pull the twine until the upper edge of the guage touches the bottom of the loop and trap the twine under the thumb.

Left to right
Figures 1.88–95

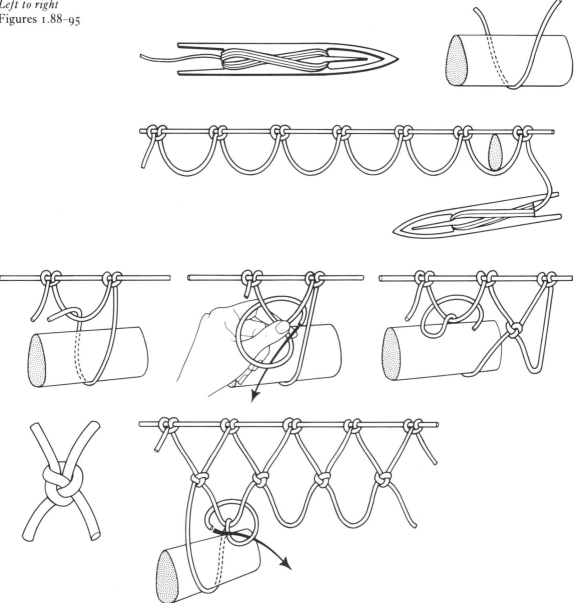

Pass the needle across the thumb behind the half mesh, left to right and down through the loop in front. Pull tight (Fig. 1.92). Do not release your thumb until the knot is formed. Work across the half mesh loops making one row of complete diamonds. Fig. 1.93 shows the first complete mesh and Fig. 1.94 the sheep-bend, the knot you have been using.

Having completed one row of mesh, measure a full mesh at the left-hand end and repeat the procedure, working from left to right (Fig. 1.95). This time the needle is passed behind the loop from right to left.

To reduce or increase the width of the net you can pick up two loops at a time

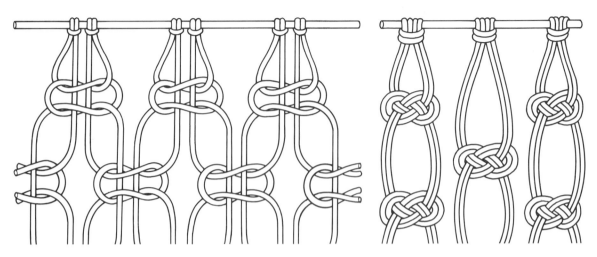

Left to right
Figures 1.96 & 97

at regular intervals or add two loops onto single half mesh loops. In the case of a circular net it is necessary to reverse direction.

A more elaborate type of netting suitable for use as a room-divider, can be made by using the square-knot (Fig. 1.96).

Fig. 1.97 illustrates a door-hanging made with the Josephine knot and doubled cords.

To cover the variations and scope of the many hundreds of knots and macramé patterns, would indeed need many volumes; thus, in this short chapter, the writer has only attempted to show a few of the simple and practical knots which can be made with a little practice and it is hoped that the pleasure and fascination of trying a few of them will encourage the reader to explore the considerable scope and artistic skill which can be achieved.

Glossary

Yarn A number of fibres twisted together.

Strands A number of yarns twisted together.

Ply A term meaning strands, used in reference to jute twines.

Unlay Unravel.

Working end The end of the rope which is passed round the knot pattern.

Standing part The part of the rope which is not worked into a knot.

Tail end The loose end of rope at the opposite end to the working end.

Loop A curve in a rope where the ends may touch, but do not cross.

Round turn A circle of rope where the ends cross.

Cross-over Where a rope crosses itself or another rope.

Bight The middle part of a rope, often semi-circular.

Terminal knot Knot at the end of a rope.

Hitch Tying a rope to another object.

Bend Joining two ropes.

Whipping A cord or twine wrapped round one or more strands of rope to hold them together.

CHERRY WARD

Crochet

THE WORD crochet comes from the French word meaning 'hook'. The craft is very old and was used traditionally for lacy designs. It was popular in the eighteenth and nineteenth centuries, but went out of favour, with other Victoriana, early in this century. Recently it has come into fashion again, in new as well as traditional forms, due in part to modern synthetic yarns, which are easily washed, non-shrink and in attractive colours, suitable for fashion garments. Knitting yarns are very popular today, together with other materials. String, for instance would be better than wool for making table-mats, but, of course, it must be pliable.

Materials and equipment

crochet hooks—various sizes	pins
crochet prong	safety pins
crewel needle	scissors
cotton, yarn—various ply	tape measure

Sizes of hooks for crochet in wool

English (old size-disc)		2	3	4	5	6	7	8	9	10	11	12	13	14
American		K/10¼	J/10	I/9	H/8	H/8	G6	F/5	E/4	D/3	C2	B/1		
Continental mm (metric)	7½	7	6.5	6	5.5	5	4.5	4	3.5	3.25	3/2.75	2.5	2.25	2

Sizes of hooks for crochet in cotton

English (old size-steel)	0	1	–	1½	2	2½	3	3½	4	4½	5	5½	6	6½	7	7½
American	1	2	3	4	5	6	–	7	8	9	10	11	12	13	14	–
Continental mm (metric)	2.50	–	–	2.00	–	1.75	–	1.50	–	1.25	–	1.00	–	0.75	0.60	–

Basic techniques

Crochet is very simple to learn and quick and easy to do. Once the basic stitches are mastered new patterns can be invented with ease.

As with knitting, tension is all important; one stitch per inch too many or too few will drastically alter the size of the finished work. Where an exact yarn advised in a pattern is not available, it is very necessary to test your tension before beginning, as the substitute may result in the work not being of the same measurements. Different yarns vary in length and weight per ball, so more or less may be required than stated in the pattern. If your tension is too tight, use a size larger hook, but, if too loose, a size smaller is advisable.

Abbreviations used in crochet instructions:

English		*American*
ch.	chain	chain
d.c.	double crochet	single crochet
s.s.	slip stitch or single crochet	slip stitch
h.tr.	half treble	half double crochet
tr.	treble	double crochet
d.tr.	double treble	treble crochet
tr.tr.	triple treble	double treble
yoh.	yarn over hook	
dyt.	draw yarn through	
lp.	loop	
sp.	space	
inc.	increase	
dec.	decrease	
st.	stitch	
tog.	together	
cl.	cluster	
gr.	group	
patt.	pattern	
rep.	repeat	
( )	repeat instructions number of times indicated	

STITCHES

Slip Loop Hold the yarn firmly between the thumb and forefinger of the left hand, the end of the yarn coming from the left. Make a circle of yarn by crossing it over the part being held (Fig. 2.1). Now, taking the hook like a pen in the right hand, pull the yarn through the circle. This will give you a slip loop to start the chain. Pull gently until you have a loose loop.

Position of hands With the yarn coming from the ball on the right, and still grasping the hook and loop with the left thumb and forefinger, take the yarn under the forefinger, over the raised second finger and under the third and fourth fingers of the left hand (Fig. 2.2). If necessary, to increase the tension on the yarn as it is worked, it may be advisable to pass the yarn around the fourth finger (Fig. 2.2 & 3).

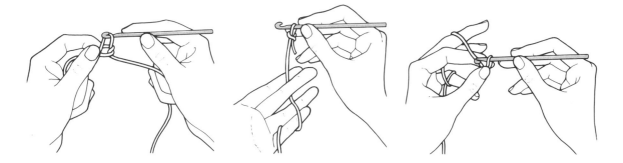

Left to right
Figures 2.1–3

Chain This is made as a foundation for all work. Make sure that it is loose as the hook has to go into each ch.st. and a tight ch. will make working very difficult.

To start the ch., form a slip lp. Now, holding the hook in the right hand as before, take it under the yarn, yoh., dyt. lp. (Fig. 2.4). *Do not pull tightly*. Repeat until the required number of ch. have been made, lifting the left thumb and forefinger after every few ch. to hold work firmly. Complete 20 ch. as a foundation row.

Slip stitch With 1 lp. on hook, insert the hook under the top two threads of the next st., yoh., dyt. both st. and lp., thus giving a ch. st. lying on top of the work (Fig. 2.5).

Double Crochet You will notice that each ch. st. of the foundation row is made up of three threads. Insert hook under the two top threads of 2nd ch. from hook, going from the front of the work, yoh. as in ch. (Fig. 2.6), dyt., to give 2 lp. on the hook, yoh., dyt. 2 lp. to give 1 lp. on hook. This is one complete d.c.

Work 1 d.c. into each ch. to the end of the row. Make 1 ch.—this will count as the 1st st. of the next row and will serve to keep the row ends at the same height as the rest of the work. With the other side of the work facing you, d.c. into the 2nd st. from the hook, then d.c. into each d.c. until you reach the end of the row.

Left to right
Figures 2.4–6

Half Treble Having completed a row of d.c., make 2 turning ch.; turn, yoh., insert hook into 2nd d.c. of previous row, yoh., dyt. to give 3 lp. on hook, yoh.

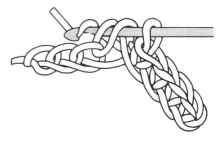

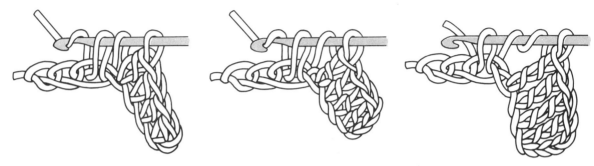

Left to right
Figures 2.7–9

(Fig. 2.7), dyt. 3 lp. to give 1 lp. on hook. This is 1 h.tr.; h.tr. into each d.c. to end of row. Make 1 h.tr. in 1st turning ch. of previous row.

Treble Proceeding to the next stitch, the tr., make 3 turning ch.; yoh., insert hook into 2nd h.tr. of previous row, yoh. (Fig. 2.8), dyt. to give 3 lp. on hook, (yoh., dyt. 2 lp.) 2 times to give 1 lp. on hook; tr. into each h.tr. to end of row. Make 3 turning ch. to begin next row of tr.

Double Treble With a row of tr. as the foundation row, make 4 turning ch.; (yoh.) 2 times, insert hook into 2nd tr. of previous row, yoh., dyt. to give 4 lp. on hook (Fig. 2.9), (yoh., dyt. 2 lp.) 3 times to give 1 lp. on hook and to complete d.tr.; d.tr. into each tr. to end of row.

Triple Treble Having completed a row of d.tr., make 5 turning ch., (yoh.) 3 times, insert into 2nd d.tr. of previous row, yoh., dyt. to give 5 lp. on hook, (yoh., dyt. 2 lp.) 4 times to give 1 lp. on hook and to complete tr.tr.; tr.tr. into each d.tr. to end of row.

Always insert the hook under the two top threads of st. in the previous row, unless directed otherwise in the pattern.

When starting a new ball of yarn, commence at the beginning of a row. The surplus can be used for any sewing up necessary. Besides evenness, which comes with practise, neatness is essential in making up your work, for a professional finish.

Projects

COLOURFUL CROCHET BAG

Materials Odd balls of double knitting yarn: 2 balls nasturtium, 2 balls linden green, 1 ball loam brown. Hook: 4mm (English No. 8).

1st row—With brown, make foundation row of 62 ch. 1 d.c. into 2nd ch. from hook, 1 d.c. into each ch. to end of row, 1 ch. to turn.
2nd row—1 d.c. into 2nd d.c. of previous row, 1 d.c. into each d.c. to end, making last d.c. into top of turning ch. at beginning of first row, 3 ch., turn.
3rd row—Join in nasturtium and, into 2nd d.c. of previous row, work 1 tr. Work 1 tr. in each d.c. to end, 1 tr. in top of turning ch., 3 ch., turn.
4th row—Repeat 2nd row.

5th row—Join in linden green and repeat 3rd row.

6th row—Repeat 4th row, with only 1 turning ch. at end of last row.

Picking up yarn at left side of work, in the same colour sequence, rep. last 6 rows (2 brown d.c., 2 nasturtium tr., 2 linden green tr.) 24 times. Work 1 row brown d.c., 2 rows nasturtium tr. and finally 2 rows brown d.c., leaving a small amount of yarn to pull through last st. and fasten off neatly.

Making up Fold work in half and join the two open sides together as evenly as possible using d.c. For a handle, either make two 45 cm (18 in) twisted cords in brown with fringed ends or the same lengths in ch. using double yarn; or purchase a cord. Divide the tops of each side of the bag evenly into three, mark with pins, and sew on the handles, as marked.

SQUARE CUSHION

Materials 3 × 40 g balls double crepe in loam brown, 2 balls camel, 1 ball oyster, small quantity orange. Hook: 4 mm (English No. 8) and a 45 cm (18 in) square cushion pad.

Starting with orange, make 8 ch. and join with s.s.

1st round—3 ch. (*yoh., hook into ring, yoh., draw through ring, yoh. dyt. 2 lp.) twice, yoh. dyt. 3 lp., 5 ch. Rep. (*) 3 times, yoh. dyt. 4 lp., thus forming a cl. Make 6 more cl. with 5 ch. between each, 5 ch., s.s. into 1st cl. (8 cl. in all), s.s. under ch. between 1st 2 cl.

2nd round—Join in oyster (first contrast) and work 3 ch. 2 cl., as on 1st round, with 5 ch. between, into 5 ch. sp., 2 ch. 3 tr. 2 ch. into next 5 ch. sp. Continue thus to end of round and join to top of 1st cl. with s.s.

3rd round—s.s. into 5 ch. sp. (1 cl. 5 ch. 1 cl. into same sp., 2 ch. 2 tr. in 2 ch. sp., 3 tr. into 3 tr., 2 tr. into 2 ch. sp., 4 ch.) Rep. all round, joining, as before, with s.s. into top of cl.

4th round—s.s. into 5 ch. sp. (1 cl. 5 ch. 1 cl. into same sp., 2 ch. 2 tr. into 2 ch. sp., 7 tr. into 7 tr. of previous round, 2 tr. 2 ch.) Rep. all round. Join with s.s.

5th round—As 4th round but with 11 tr. into 11 tr.

6th round—s.s. into 5 ch. sp. (1 cl. 5 ch. 1 cl. into same sp., 2 ch., 1 tr. in 2 ch. sp., 6 tr. into 6 tr. of previous round, miss 1 tr., 1 cl. 3 ch. 1 cl. in next tr., miss 1 tr., 6 tr. into 6 tr., 1 tr. into 2 ch. sp.) Rep. all round and join with s.s. Rep. this round twice. Change to next contrast (camel) for 7 rounds, then work 8 rounds in loam brown—23 rounds in all. Fasten off neatly and make the second side to match.

Making up With right sides outside, join three sides together with orange, 1 d.c. into a tr. from each side, and working 2 d.c. into 2 ch. sp., 3 d.c. into 3 ch. sp. at corners. Insert the foam pad, after covering with suitable material, and join the fourth sides as for the other three. Finally, working from left to right—backwards—make 1 d.c. into each d.c. of previous round. This is cord or crab-stitch. Fasten off neatly.

PALE GREEN JUMPER

Materials 5 × 50g balls 4-ply wool. Hook: 3.5mm (English No. 9).

Tension 2 patterns 7.5 cm (3 in) width. 7 pattern rows 7.5 cm (3 in) depth.

Size Bust 86 cm (34 in), length from nape of neck 63 cm (25 in), adjustable.

To form the welt make 10 ch.; 1 d.c. into 2nd ch. from hook., d.c. into each ch. to end, 1 ch., turn. Work 1 d.c. onto back lp. only of each d.c., 1 ch., turn. Rep. until 72 rows have been worked. This completes the welt but do not break yarn. Turn sideways and work 73 d.c. into the side edge, 5 ch., turn. Right side of work—1 tr. into 1st d.c., (*miss 2 d.c., 5 tr. into next d.c., miss 2 d.c., 1 tr. 2 ch. 1 tr. into next d.c.) Rep. (*) to end, 3 ch., turn.

1st row—2 tr. into 2 ch. sp., (*1 tr. 2 ch. 1 tr. into centre tr. of 5 of previous row, 5 tr. into next 2 ch. sp.) Rep. (*) to last 2 ch. sp., 3 tr., 5 ch., turn.

2nd row—1 tr. into 1st d.c., (*5 tr. into 2 ch. sp., 1 tr. 2 ch. 1 tr. in centre tr. of 5 of previous row.) Rep. (*) to last 3 tr., 1 tr. 2 ch. 1 tr., all into last tr. These 2 rows form the patt.

For front of jumper continue in pattern until work measures 40 cm (15½ in) from start, ending on a 2nd row (length of garment may be adjusted here), 5 ch., turn.

Next row—Into 3rd ch. from hook, work 2 tr. Continue in patt. to end of row, 5 ch., turn.

Next row—1 tr. in 1st of 5 ch. Continue in patt. to end. These 2 inc. give an extra ½ patt. each end of row. Continue in patt. for 12.5 cm (5 in) more, ending on wrong side of work.

Next row—Work 4 patt., 1 tr. 2 ch. 1 tr. into 3rd of 5 tr. gr., 1 tr. into 2 ch. sp., turn.

Next row—3 ch., 5 tr. into 2 ch. sp., and continue in patt. to end of row.

Continue until 62 cm (24½ in) are completed, ending on wrong side of work, then shape shoulder. S.s. to middle tr. of 1st 5 tr. gr., 3 ch., continue in patt. to end of row. Fasten off. To complete other shoulder, miss 3 complete patt. and 5 tr. gr. Rejoin yarn to next 2 ch. sp., work 3 ch. 1 tr. 2 ch. 1 tr. into 3rd of 5 tr. gr. Continue in patt. to end of row.

Proceed as for other shoulder, reversing shaping.

Front of garment. Work exactly as back until 11 rows have been worked after sleeve shaping.

Next row—Keeping edge of work as in previous rows, work 4 complete patt. only, and continue on these 4 patt. for 9 more rows, shaping shoulder to match that of the back.

Work other side of neck to correspond. Fasten all ends securely and neatly.

Making up Neatly sew up side and shoulder seams.

Neck: round the neck, with right side of work facing, from right of back of neck work 1 d.c. into each of 5 tr. gr., 1 d.c. in 1 tr., 2 d.c. into 2 ch. sp., 1 d.c. in 1 tr. Rep. to left side of back.

At side of neck opening work 2 d.c. in each row end. Continue front of neck as back and other side to correspond with the first one. Join with s.s. Turn with 1 ch., 1 d.c. into each d.c. to last d.c. of side neck, (*hook into last d.c., yoh. dyt., into 1st d.c. of front neck yoh., dyt., yoh. and dyt. 3 lp., making 1 d.c. of 2 corner d.c.) Rep. (*) in reverse at the other front corner and work the rest of round in d.c. over d.c. of previous round. Complete neck with 2 more similar rounds. Fasten off and sew end in neatly.

Sleevebands: join yarn at underarm seam and work 2 d.c. in the end of each row, right round the armhole, s.s. into 1st d.c., 1 ch., turn. Work 1 d.c. into each d.c. of previous round on the next 3 rounds, omitting 1 ch. on last round. Fasten off and neaten ends. Press garment under a dry cloth with a cool iron.

MATINEE COAT

Materials 4 balls 3-ply wool. Hook: 3 mm (English No. 10) 0.9 m (1 yd) baby ribbon.

Tension 2 patt., 6 rows measured over skirt patt. 5 cm (2 in) square.

Size 50 cm (20 in) chest, length from shoulder 24 cm ($9\frac{1}{2}$ in), sleeve seam 12.5 cm (5 in).

Make 49 ch., 1 d.c. in 2nd ch. from hook, 1 d.c. in each ch. to end (47 d.c.), 1 ch., turn.

Yoke: Continue as follows:

1st row—10 d.c., 2 d.c. into each of next 2 d.c., 1 d.c. in next d.c., 2 d.c. in each of next 2 d.c., 1 d.c. in each of next 17 d.c., 2 d.c. in each of next 2 d.c., 1 d.c. in next d.c., 2 d.c. in each 2 d.c., 1 d.c. in each d.c. to end, 1 ch., turn.

2nd row—11 d.c., 2 d.c. into each of next 2 d.c., 1 d.c. in each of next 3 d.c., 2 d.c. into each of next 2 d.c., 1 d.c. in each of next 19 d.c., 2 d.c. into each of next 2 d.c., 1 d.c. into each of next 3 d.c., 2 d.c. into each of next 2 d.c., 1 d.c. into each d.c. to end. 1 ch., turn.

3rd row—12 d.c., 2 d.c. into each of next 2 d.c., 1 d.c. into each of next 5 d.c., 2 d.c. into each of next 2 d.c., 1 d.c. in each of next 21 d.c., 2 d.c. into each of next 2 d.c., 1 d.c. in each of next 5 d.c., 2 d.c. into each of next 2 d.c., 1 d.c. into each d.c. to end, 1 ch., turn.

Continue thus until the 20th row has been worked (196 d.c.).

Next row—1 d.c. into each of 30 d.c., miss 41 d.c. for armhole, 55 d.c., miss 41 d.c. for 2nd armhole, 30 d.c., 1 ch., turn.

Skirt: 1 d.c. in each of 2 d.c., 2 d.c. in each d.c. to last 2 d.c., 1 d.c. in each (226 d.c.), 2 ch., turn.

1st patt. row—Miss 2 d.c. (*2 tr. 2 ch. 2 tr. all in next d.c., miss 2 d.c., h.tr. pulled up to 1 cm ($\frac{1}{2}$ in) height in next d.c.—i.e. long h.tr.) Rep. (*) to end of row, 2 ch., turn.

2nd patt. row—(*2 tr. 2 ch. 2 tr. in 2 ch. sp., long h.tr. as previous row, working this st. round h.tr. below from right to left.) Rep. (*) to end of row, 2 ch., turn.

3rd patt. row—Wrong side of work. (*2 tr. 2 ch. 2 tr. in 2 ch. sp., yoh. for h.tr., hook to back of work behind h.tr. of previous row, yoh. pull through, and complete long h.tr.) Rep. (*) to end of row, 2 ch., turn.

Rep. these last 2 rows 8 times—15 cm (6 in), working 1 turning ch. on last row. To finish off main part of matinée coat, work 1 d.c. into each tr. of previous row, 2 d.c. in each 2 ch. sp., and 1 d.c. each side of each long h.tr. On sides of skirt, work 2 d.c. over each 2 turning ch. at row ends and 1 d.c. at end of every d.c. row of side of yoke, 2 ch. at end.

Round neck: 1 tr. at base of last d.c. on side edging (2 ch. miss 2 d.c., 1 tr., in each of next 2 d.c.) Rep. to other side of neck, then complete other front to match.

Sleeves: With right side of work facing, work 2 tr. 2 ch. 2 tr. into same d.c. as 10th group of 2 tr. 2 ch. 2 tr. from front of skirt; then work up the side yoke in d.c. (miss 2 d.c. long h.tr. in next d.c., miss 2 d.c., 2 tr. 2 ch. 2 tr. in next d.c.) 7 times, 1 tr. into 1 d.c. below, on skirt, 2 ch., turn. Work 10 more rows as for skirt, finishing with d.c. edging as on skirt. Sew sleeve seam neatly.

Work second sleeve to correspond. Use 50 cm (20 in) of ribbon to slot round neck, leaving 19 cm ($7\frac{1}{2}$ in) for each sleeve and finishing with a bow.

HAIRPIN CROCHET TABLE CENTRE

Materials 2 balls white crochet cotton No. 10. Hook: 1.75 mm (English No. $3\frac{1}{2}$). Crochet prong 60 mm (English No. $2\frac{1}{2}$).

Hairpin crochet is made in strips, which are then crocheted together.

Method Make a slip lp. with yarn. Holding crochet prong with open end upwards, slide lp. to the centre of bottom bar and pull, leaving it sufficiently slack to slide around the bar. Lift the yarn upwards between the parallel bars and, while holding the slip lp. firmly between thumb and forefinger of left hand, take the yarn to the front of the left bar, round the back of it, and then between the bars, to the front of the right bar and round it to the back. Now placing the yarn over the left hand, in the usual position for crochet, take the crochet hook under the bottom strand, pull the strand which is by your middle finger underneath the 2 strands which are going round the side bars to the front and lock with a s.s. With the hook of the crochet hook facing you, slide it round until upright, pull to a horizontal position and, holding the hook in your right hand, turn the left bar of the crochet prong towards the back and the right, so that the hook is now in the working position, and the yarn round the right-hand bar. Placing the hook under the left front lp., pull the yarn through from the back, yoh. dyt., yoh., and dyt. 2 lp. on hook (d.c.). Now (with hook facing left between the prongs again, turn the left bar to the back and right, hook under top left lp., dyt. from the back again, yoh. and complete d.c.). Repeat until sufficient lp. have been worked on each side to use the strip for the article you wish to make. Lp. should be joined twisted, as when on the crochet prong. To start the centre strip for the table centre, work 66 lp. each side of the central d.c. making sure not to pull the prongs together as the work grows. Fasten off the working end, remove the strip from the crochet prong and join ends securely and neatly together. Using a crewel- or wool-needle and yarn, dyt. lp. on one side of strip to form the centre of work and finish off securely as before.

2nd strip—Work 132 lp. each side of centre d.c. Finish off and join 1st and last d.c. to form a circle. Work tog. the lp. from the 2nd side of 1st strip and 1st side of 2nd strip, by taking 2 lp. from centre strip on to hook and 4 lp. from 2nd strip and pulling them through the 1st 2 lp. From the 1st strip, slip 2 lp. on to the hook again and pull through the 4 lp. on hook, then take 4 more lp. from 2nd strip and pull through the 2 lp. on hook. Continue thus until all the lp. have been joined. Sew the last gr. in place. The lp. on the other side of the 2nd strip are left until the 3rd strip is ready. Joining will be easier if these 132 lp. are put on small safety-pins in 11 groups of 12.

3rd strip—Make 176 lp. either side of central d.c. using safety pins to hold them in 11 gr. of 16. Form a circle as before and fasten securely. To join the 2nd and 3rd strips tog., start at central d.c. of 2nd strip with a d.c. between 2 of the gr. of 12. Take tog. with 1 d.c., removing each safety-pin as you work the lp. from it; 16 lp. from 3rd strip (10 ch. 1 d.c. over central d.c. on 3rd strip, before the next gr. of 16 lp. held tog. with 1 d.c., 12 lp. from 2nd strip, 10 ch. 1 d.c. over central d.c. on 2nd strip, before the next gr., 1 d.c. into next 16 lp. on 3rd strip). Rep. until the circle can be completed with s.s. into 1st d.c. 2nd edge of 3rd strip—(Take 2 twisted lp. tog. with a d.c., 3 ch.) rep. to end and join circle.

4th strip—Make 440 lp. each side of central d.c. (Safety-pins holding 20 lp. each would facilitate counting.)

First edge of 4th strip—(Take 5 twisted lp. tog. with a d.c., 3 ch.) rep. to end and join up circle. Work 3rd and 4th strips tog. with a lengthened s.s. in 2nd of 3 ch. in each strip, 3 ch. Rep. to complete circle and join.

Second edge of 4th strip—(Take 5 twisted lp. tog. with a d.c., 4 ch.), rep. all round and join as before. Do not turn work.

Next round—(3 d.c. into each 4 ch. lp., 1 d.c. in each of 5 lp. gr.), rep. all round. Join with s.s. Do not turn work.

Next round—(3 ch., miss 1 d.c., s.s. in back only of next d.c.), rep. all round. Join and neaten.

To finish, pin work out wrong side up and, covering with a damp cloth, press with a fairly hot iron.

3

CHERRY WARD

Tatting

THIS IS another old craft. It was used over the centuries in Brussels, France and the Near East to make beautiful lace and is mentioned in Chaucer's *Canterbury Tales*, written nearly six hundred years ago.

Materials and equipment

shuttle
crochet hook
threads of linen, cotton, or mercerised cotton, from fine to medium coarse
pins

Tatting is made with a special shuttle, examples of which, made of abalone shell and of ivory, are in various collections in museums in both Europe and Asia. More recent examples are of bone, tortoiseshell and, most recent of all, plastic, and some made of metal have a hook incorporated at one end. Most of the plastic ones are sold with a separate hook for joining one part of the work to another. Threads of linen, cotton or mercerised cotton, from very fine to medium coarse, are suitable for working. The size of thread will vary the appearance of the finished article from very dainty to more sturdy for constantly used and washed articles like pillowcases.

Basic techniques

Abbreviations used in tatting instructions:

d.s.	double stitch	RW.	reverse work
p.	picot	sp.	space
l.p.	long picot	ch.	chain
sm.p.	small picot	tog.	together
sep.	separated	( )	repeat instructions number of times stated
r.	ring		
sm.r.	small ring	rep.	repeat
l.r.	large ring	sep.	separated
cl.	close		

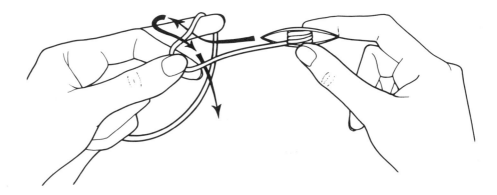

Figure 3.1

PREPARING THE SHUTTLE

To start, wind a fairly coarse thread, crochet cotton No. 10 or similar, evenly on to the shuttle, not allowing the thread to protrude over the edges when full. Unwind about 38 cm (15 in) of thread from the shuttle, so that the end comes from the back right-hand side. Hold the shuttle in the right hand, with the thumb underneath and the forefinger on top.

Below
Figures 3.2–7

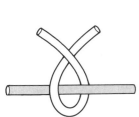

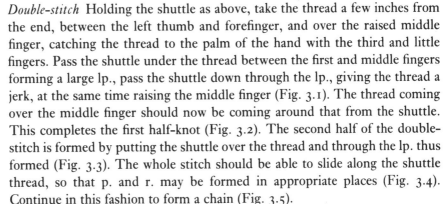

STITCHES

Tatting is worked with one kind of stitch only, made up of two halves which together form the double stitch (d.s.). It is decorated with picots (p.).

Double-stitch Holding the shuttle as above, take the thread a few inches from the end, between the left thumb and forefinger, and over the raised middle finger, catching the thread to the palm of the hand with the third and little fingers. Pass the shuttle under the thread between the first and middle fingers forming a large lp., pass the shuttle down through the lp., giving the thread a jerk, at the same time raising the middle finger (Fig. 3.1). The thread coming over the middle finger should now be coming around that from the shuttle. This completes the first half-knot (Fig. 3.2). The second half of the double-stitch is formed by putting the shuttle over the thread and through the lp. thus formed (Fig. 3.3). The whole stitch should be able to slide along the shuttle thread, so that p. and r. may be formed in appropriate places (Fig. 3.4). Continue in this fashion to form a chain (Fig. 3.5).

Picots These are made by leaving a space between 2 d.s. (Fig. 3.6). The d.s. is made to slide along the thread, so that any space will form a lp. or p. (Fig. 3.7). This sliding is achieved by giving a jerk to the thread, causing it to turn

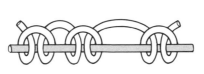

from the thread held over the fingers to that coming from the shuttle. This part of the d.s. is the most important and may require practise to perfect. Having once mastered this half of the stitch, the rest is easily acquired.

When the double-stitch has been perfected it will be possible to make a simple edging for a handkerchief.

Projects

HANDKERCHIEF EDGING

Materials A fine cotton, white or coloured, would be most effective and dainty.

This consists of a series of r. made as follows:

1st ring—3 d.s., (*p., 3 d.s.) Rep. 4 times. Close the r. by pulling the yarn, thus causing the d.s. and p. to slide along until they form a circle.

2nd ring—Leave a gap of 1 cm ($\frac{1}{2}$ in) thread from the last r., 3 d.s. Join to last p. of previous r. by inserting hook into p. Pull strand of new r. through as a lp., pass shuttle through and draw thread up—this counts as 1 st. of a d.s.—complete this d.s. by working the 2nd half as usual, and finish r. as in previous r. by working from *. Repeat 2nd r. for length required to go round the handkerchief, cut thread, leaving sufficient to sew together, and neaten ends. Sew neatly to handkerchief.

The next step is to work with 2 threads, so that both r. and ch. may be worked. The 2 threads may be of the same or different colours, as preferred. The shuttle thread and the thread from the ball of yarn are tied together, the one coming from the ball being used to make a chain. That thread is held between thumb and forefinger and the shuttle thread worked over it, just as if a r. was being made (Fig. 3.8). When a r. is required, the ball thread is dropped and the shuttle thread used in the ordinary way.

Figure 3.8

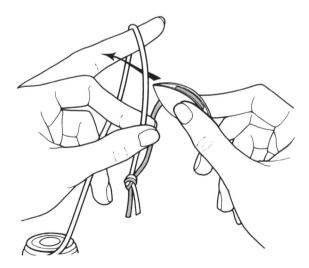

COLLAR EDGING

Materials A bought or a made collar may be used for this and a medium-sized thread, such as crochet cotton No. 20.

Tie ball and shuttle threads tog. Make a r. of 4 d.s., p., 4 d.s., 2 p., sep. by 1 p., 4 d.s., cl. RW. (ch. of 6 d.s., RW., 4 d.s. Join to last p. in previous row, 4 d.s., 2 p., sep. by 1 p., 4 d.s., p., 4 d.s., cl., RW.). Rep. for length required and attach neatly to collar, having sewn in ends neatly.

EDGING FOR PILLOW CASE

Materials 2 balls crochet cotton No. 20 or similar thickness will be required for a bold design and a bought pillow case, or a made one, into the side seams of which the beginning and end of the edging may be sewn for neatness.

1st row—Tie ball and shuttle threads tog. Make a r. of 6 d.s., p., 6 d.s., cl., RW.; ch. of 5 d.s., p., 5 d.s., 3 p., sep. by 1 d.s., 5 d.s., p., 5 d.s., RW.; r. of 6 d.s., join to p. on previous r., 6 d.s., cl.; r. of 6 d.s., p., 6 d.s., cl., RW.; ch. of 5 d.s. Join to ball thread to last p. on previous ch., 5 d.s., 3 p., sep. by 1 d.s., 5 d.s., p., 5 d.s., RW.; r. of 6 d.s. Join to p. of last r., 6 d.s., cl. Rep. to 46 cm (18 in) or length required.
Tie ends, cut, and sew in neatly on wrong side.
2nd row—Tie ball and shuttle threads tog. Attach to base of 1st r. of previous row, ch. of (2 d.s., p.) 8 times, 2 d.s. Join shuttle thread to space between 2 r. on previous row. Rep. to end of row.
3rd row—Tie ball and shuttle thread tog. Join ball thread to 4th p. of previous row, 8 d.s., r. of 3 d.s., 3 p. sep. by 3 d.s., cl. (*r. of 3 d.s., join to previous row through last p., 2 d.s., 6 p. sep. by 2 d.s., 3 d.s., cl.; r. of 3 d.s. Join to last p. of previous r., 3 d.s., 2 p. sep. by 3 d.s., 3 d.s., 3 d.s., cl.; ch. of 8 d.s. Join to 2nd p. of previous r., 3 d.s., p., 3 d.s. cl.) Rep. to end of row. Cut thread and sew in all ends neatly on wrong side of work. When sewn to pillow case it is neater to sew the ends of the edging into the top of the side seams of the case.

TWO-COLOUR MOTIF

Motifs are useful for making up mats, tray cloths, cheval sets, chair and settee backs and other items by adjusting the number of motifs used. Also they may be made in a single colour or in two.

Materials This motif was made in white and mauve crochet cotton No. 20 but similar medium-sized cotton and other colours may be substituted.

1st round—Tie ball and shuttle threads tog., (r. of 8 d.s., 4 p., sep. by 3 d.s., 8 d.s., cl., RW.) 3 times. Join to base of 1st r., tie ends, cut and neaten.
2nd round—Tie ball and shuttle threads tog., (r. of 6 d.s. Join to last p. of previous round. 6 d.s., cl., RW., ch. of 5 d.s., p., 5 d.s., RW., r. of 6 d.s. Join to next p. of same r., 6 d.s., cl.) 2 times, RW., ch. of 5 d.s. Join to corresponding p. on 1st motif, 5 d.s., RW., r. of 6 d.s. Join to next p. on 1st motif, 5 d.s., RW.,

r. of 6 d.s. Join to 1st p. on next r. on 1st row of 2nd motif, 6 d.s., cl., RW., ch. of 5 d.s. Join to next p. on 1st motif, 5 d.s., RW, and complete as for 1st motif. When joined into sets of 4 motifs, 6 ch. can be worked at centre from corner p. to p. forming a square of ch.

TABLE CENTRE

Materials 2 balls crochet cotton No. 20 in golden yellow, or other chosen colour.

1st round—Tie ball and shuttle threads tog. Make r. of 8 d.s., 1 lp., 8 d.s., cl., RW., ch. of 6 d.s., 3 p. sep. by 3 d.s., 6 d.s. (RW., r. of 8 d.s., join to lp. of previous r., 8 d.s., cl., RW., ch. of 6 d.s., 3 p. sep. by 3 d.s., 6 d.s.) 4 times. Join to beginning of 1st ch., tie, cut ends and sew them in neatly on the wrong side of work.

2nd round—Tie ball and shuttle threads tog. Join threads to 1st p. of any ch. of previous round, (ch. of 3 d.s., 5 p. sep. by 3 d.s., join to 3rd p. of same ch. of previous round), rep. all round. Join, tie, cut and neaten ends.

3rd round—Join threads to 2nd p. of any ch. in ch. of previous round (ch. of 5 d.s., 1 p., 5 d.s., join to 4th p. of same ch. of previous round) rep. all round. Join, tie, cut and neaten ends.

4th round—Tie ball and shuttle threads tog., (r. of 10 d.s., join to any p. of previous round, 10 d.s., cl.; r. of 10 d.s., join to next p. in same round, 10 d.s., cl.; RW., ch. of 5 d.s., 5 p. sep. by 3 d.s., 5 d.s.) rep. all round. Join, tie, cut and neaten ends.

5th round—Tie ball and shuttle threads tog. and attach ball thread to last lp. of any ch. of previous round, (ch. of 8 d.s., p., 8 d.s., join to 1st p. in next ch., ch. of 5 d.s., 5 p. sep. by 3 d.s., 5 d.s., join to last p. of same ch. of previous round) rep. all round. Join, tie, cut and neaten ends.

6th round—Tie ball and shuttle threads tog. Join to centre p. of 5 on previous round, (ch. of 10 d.s., RW., r. of 8 d.s., p., 8 d.s., cl.; 2nd r. of 8 d.s., p., 8 d.s., cl., RW., 10 d.s., join to p. in next ch. of previous round) rep. all round. Join, tie cut and neaten ends.

7th round—Tie ball and shuttle threads tog. Join to any p. of previous round, (ch. of 6 d.s., lp., 6 d.s., join to next p. of previous round) rep. to end of round. Tie ends, cut and sew in neatly.

8th round—Tie ball and shuttle threads tog., join to any lp. of previous round, (ch. of 15 d.s., join to next lp. of previous round) rep. to end of round. Do not cut and tie ends, but continue thus:

9th round—(ch. of 3 d.s., 6 p. sep. by 3 d.s., 3 d.s., join to next lp. of previous round, pulling ch. up to fit snugly over 15 d.s. ch. of previous round. Join to next lp. of previous round) rep. right round work. Tie ends, cut and sew in on wrong side of work to neaten.

To finish, pin work out, wrong side uppermost, and press under a damp cloth.

4 Bobbin Lace

JEAN PEGG

LACE HAS been in existence since the ancient Egyptians. It was first found in the tombs excavated at Herkaleopolis Magna. Fragments of two distinct types were discovered—one a kind of netting, in which each crossing was fastened by a knot. 'Filet' lace originated from this. The second type consisted of twisted threads without knots and it appears to be from this that bobbin lace originated.

References to lace are made in the Old Testament—for example Exodus *XXXVIII*, with reference to the making of the ephod:

And they shall bind the breast plate by rings thereof into rings of the ephod with a lace of blue. . . .

The earliest pieces of lace found in Great Britain were discovered when a Scandinavian barrow near Wareham in Dorset, was excavated. They were made in gold thread, measuring 10×6 cm ($4 \times 2\frac{1}{2}$ in) and with a lozenge pattern; this design was used by the Danes in borders for edging clothes.

Little is known about bobbin lace until the sixteenth century, although needle-made lace was made earlier. Queen Elizabeth I favoured bone lace to adorn her sumptuous gowns so the fashion of wearing bone lace was soon adopted by courts throughout Europe.

The survivors of the slaughter of the Huguenots in 1572 came to Britain. They settled in Buckingham and Devon and eventually Honiton lace was developed, the emigrants teaching the local people. The lace industry continued to thrive. Daniel Defoe wrote in 1724 of Blandford:

This City is chiefly famous for making the finest bone lace in England and when they showed us some so exquisitely fine as I think I never saw better in Flanders, France or Italy. They value it at £30 per yard.

The year 1803 saw the invention of John Heathcoate's lace machine. This invention put an end to the hand-made lace cottage industry. However, Queen Victoria favoured hand-made lace. It is estimated that her wedding gown cost £1000 and its execution occupied many Honiton lace-workers. I have in my possession a sprig of lace made by one of the lace-workers.

Lace-schools were found all over the east Midlands suring the nineteenth century. Sadly, the last one closed its doors in the 1920s. Fortunately a small band of dedicated lace-workers continued to produce beautiful laces and to teach this ancient craft and today we have a growing interest in lace-making throughout Great Britain.

Lace is not a complicated craft and, if taken in easy steps, progress will soon be made.

Materials and equipment

lace pillow	threads
bobbins	pin cushion
berry pins	patterns
brass pins	scissors
fine crochet hook	working cloths

THE LACE PILLOW

To make a round pillow you will require: a piece of hardboard 40 cm (16 in) diameter; two pieces of calico 42 cm (16½ in) in diameter; chopped straw or hay; outer cover of a plain colour (green, blue, brown); a piece of blue or green felt 16 cm (8 in) square; two working-cloths 30 cm (12 in) square—the same colour as the outer cover.

Sew up the calico half-way round. Slip the board inside and sew up but leave a small opening. Stuff the pillow with straw or hay until it is very hard, then sew up the opening.

Make the outer cover in the same way. Slip the pillow inside and sew up the cover. The pillow is now ready for dressing.

Pin the felt square in the centre of the pillow, pin the parchment or lace pattern on to the felt and place a working cloth half-way down the pattern (Fig. 4.1). Be sure to have a small pin cushion attached to the pillow filled with brass lace pins. The second cloth will cover the pillow when not in use.

Figure 4.1

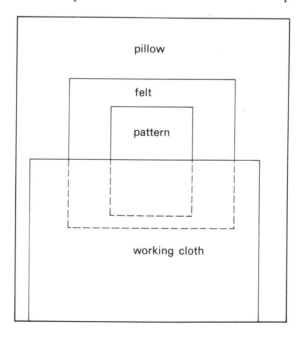

pillow

felt

pattern

working cloth

BOBBINS

Bobbins are the thread carriers and must be of good quality. You can do one of three things:

(a) You can buy bobbins. Bobbin-makers are now very plentiful in England.

(b) You can search around antique shops and auction rooms for old bobbins, which can be found but are usually very expensive. I do not recommend old bobbins for you will often find the heads are damaged and the spangles far too large and cumbersome. Although I have a fine collection of antique bobbins, I prefer to use the ones turned by my husband. These bobbins are well balanced and have excellent heads.

(c) You can make your own bobbins. This is quite a simple task and not expensive.

To make bobbins you will need 95mm ($\frac{3}{8}$in) wooden dowelling cut into 10cm (4in) lengths. Cut away until the neck of the bobbin is formed.

Carve a deep groove in the end of the bobbin to form the head. Bore a small hole in the other end through which you pass a small piece of wire; thread the wire with five beads and loop the wire together. Rub down the bobbin with fine emery paper. Do not varnish or use wood dye (Fig. 4.2 & 3).

Left to right
Figures 4.2 & 3

A bobbin case is a useful item. Take one piece of material 45cm (18in) square, fold it and sew at 2.5cm (1in) intervals.

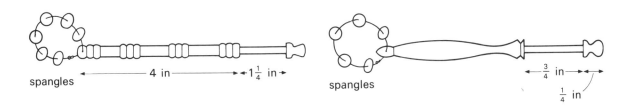

spangles — 4 in — 1¼ in →

spangles — ¾ in → ¼ in

THREADS

Linen thread is the very best for lace-making but it is very often difficult to obtain and expensive. Crochet cotton makes up well—sizes No. 20 or 40 are good to commence with.

PINS

Brass pins, fine, medium and thick will be required but ordinary dress-making pins may be used. Berry pins are useful to pin parchments on to the pillow.

A good lace-worker will not stick pins into her lace-pillow in a sloppy manner. A pin cushion is essential. The traditional shape is a strawberry, this being the lace-maker's lucky symbol. Use strawberry-coloured felt, add a green felt stalk and stuff with sheep's fleece if possible, as this will keep the pins oiled and rust-free.

PATTERNS

These are not easy to find. Prickings on parchment were much treasured by old lace-workers and were very often destroyed upon their deaths. A good teacher will supply her students with patterns but this should be done with discretion. No student should attempt patterns in advance of her capabilities. Patterns can be bought from a few firms which specialize in lace-making equipment (see list of Suppliers). Of course a good teacher will encourage students to design their own, once they have acquired the basic knowledge. Nothing is more rewarding than to design and make your own lace.

Figures 4.4 & 5

Basic techniques

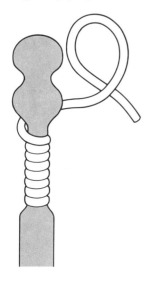

USING A PATTERN

Assemble your materials. Trace the pattern and place the tracing over pricking card or stiff card; prick out pin-holes where indicated on the diagram, using a large needle. You will find it easier to use a piece of dowelling or a cork as a holder for the needle. It is helpful to draw in the pattern faintly with pencil. Pin the pricking in the centre of the pillow, using berry pins. The following instructions are for right-handed students.

WINDING BOBBINS

Bobbins are always wound in pairs. Take a bobbin in the left hand, holding it by the shank. Lay the thread along the neck of the bobbin, holding it in place with your left thumb and commence to wind *away* from yourself (this is most important because if you wind the thread towards you the bobbin will not 'run'. Continue to wind until you have enough thread on the bobbin (approximately 0.9 m [36 in]) but do not overfill it. Do not cut the thread but secure it over the head of the bobbin with a half-hitch (Fig. 4.4 & 5). Cut off a similar length of thread from the ball. You will now have one bobbin wound and a length of thread. Take a second bobbin, wind as for the first until you have 15 cm (6 in) thread between the two bobbins and make a half-hitch. Continue to wind the bobbins until you have six pairs wound. It is a good idea when winding bobbins to place them back in the bobbin case, as this prevents any tangling.

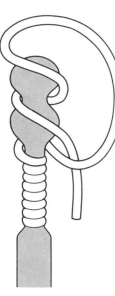

BASIC STITCHES

Lace consists of three basic stitches, whole-stitch, half-stitch and plait, which will all be found on Pattern 1 (Fig. 4.6). Prick out the pattern and wind 12 pairs of bobbins with No. 20 crochet cotton. Hang one pair of bobbins at A, B, C, D and E. These will be referred to as the passives. Hang one pair at W. These will be referred to as the workers.

Whole-stitch The workers are No. 1 and 2, the first two passives 3 and 4. Follow this sequence remembering that, as the bobbin changes its position, it changes its number:

2 over 3, 2 over 1, 4 over 2 over 3.

This is a complete whole-stitch or pass (Fig. 4.7). Continue this way through the other passive pairs; twist the worker once away from you, take a pin and pin it up at the pin-hole to the right of the pattern at a slanting outward angle. Twist the worker once more and work back along the passives. Continue to work for another five rows.

Half-stitch First cross the passive pairs right to left, now with the workers work:
2 over 3, 2 over 1, 4 over 3.
Continue to the end of the row; twist, pin up and twist and return across to the left edge. This stitch has a lattice appearance (Fig. 4.8). Continue the pattern until the plaits are reached.

Left to right
Figures 4.6–8

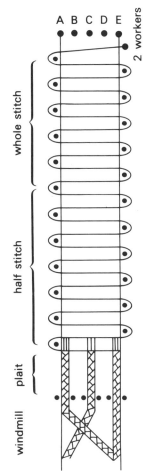

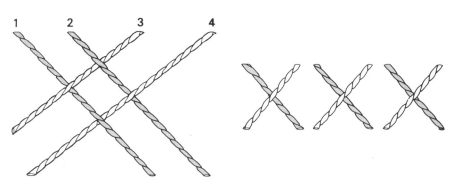

Plaits Divide the bobbins into three sets of four and pin up in the middle of each set of four bobbins. Work in half-stitch sequence one pair of bobbins— each hand gently pulling up one plait stitch worked. Repeat this sequence with the same four bobbins until the next pin-hole is reached. Now repeat with the next four bobbins. When you have reached the same length as the first plait make a windmill: work a whole-stitch with the eight bobbins, counting each pair of bobbins as one pair at 4 over 3, pin up and close with 2 over 3. Work more plait, tie off each set of four bobbins with a single knot; cut off. You have now completed the first sampler.

MOVING LACE IN THE MAKING

Work to the end of the pattern. Fold the working cloth over the bobbins and fold over the lower edge to form a pocket.
Place left hand firmly over the bobbins. Remove pins working from *top* to *bottom*. When the last pin has been removed with the left hand, gently slide the work back to the top of the pattern whilst supporting the lace already made with the right hand. Pin out the complete worked pattern, unfolding the working-cloths. Re-arrange the bobbins and commence working again. Care should be taken to pin out the foot side for at least 7.5 cm (3 in).

Figure 4.9

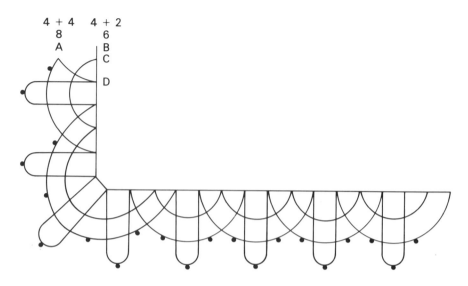

FINISHING LACE

When the required amount of lace has been made, carefully pin out one complete pattern and, with a fine crochet hook, pull one thread through the adjoining lace. A loop will have been formed. Pass the second bobbin through this loop, pull both bobbins tight; finish with a single knot and cut off. Sew ends into lace. Continue across the pattern in this manner until all the bobbins have been tied off.

LE PUY LACE (Plaited)

Pattern 2 (Fig. 4.9)

14 bobbins. No. 20 or 40 crochet cotton.

Hang eight bobbins at point A. Plait four bobbins to A and make a picot as follows: twist the left-hand pair three times. Take pin in right hand, place over twisted threads, loop pin up at A, continue to plait up tight to pin. Continue to B. Plait remaining four bobbins at A to C, return to B, plait four bobbins to C; make a windmill. This will leave two bobbins at the edge. This pair will remain at the edge. Twist four times. Continue to plait with four bobbins at C until the edge is reached.

With the edge pair counting as 1 and 2, work whole-stitch with the four bobbins from C. Pin up at a slant at D. You will now have four bobbins at the right side of the pin (outside edge) and two on the left side. Work one more whole-stitch from left to right—this will bring the two bobbins back to the edge. Continue to work the lace following the diagram. As many patterns as are required may be worked. This pattern is adaptable to both handkerchiefs and table linen, depending on the size of the thread used.

Pattern 3 (Fig. 4.10)

24 bobbins. No. 20 or 40 crochet cotton.

This lace once again is all plaits with a cloth-stitch footing.

Figure 4.10

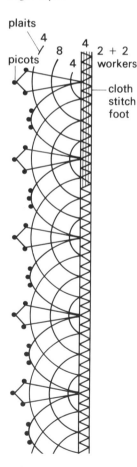

Figure 4.11

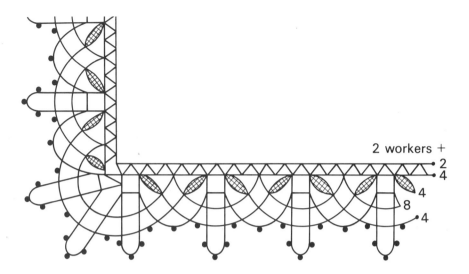

2 workers +
2
4
4
8
4

Figure 4.12

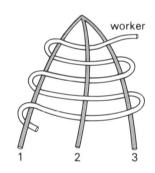

Pattern 4 (Fig. 4.11). Plaited lace with leaves
24 bobbins. No. 80 or 100 crochet cotton.
To make a leaf (Fig. 4.12), hold three bobbins in the left hand, 1 between the thumb and index finger, 2 between the index and second fingers and, missing one space, 3 between the third and fourth fingers. Rest left hand on pillow. Spread bobbins out wide. Remember your hand now acts as a loom. Take bobbin 4 as a weaver, pass it under 2, over 1. Return bobbin, spangle end *first* over 2 and under 3. Continue in this manner until the half-way stage has been reached. Move bobbin 3 to between the second and third fingers. This will help to shape the leaf. Continue to weave gradually, drawing the leaf in; to finish, lay weaver to one side, cross 3 over 2 and pin up or make a whole-stitch. It is advisable when working leaves to have a small square of black cotton material 7.5 × 7.5 cm (3 × 3 in) and to place this under the bobbins used for the leaf. This will not only protect your weaver from becoming tangled in pins already set, but you will see the leaf being formed more clearly.

You will find Bedfordshire lace, and also Cluny and Maltese lace, have leaves in their design. Of course, leaves can be found in most types of lace.

CLUNY LACE

This gets its name from laces copied from the Cluny Museum in Paris. They were of Italian origin. Cluny lace is usually made in a heavier thread but can be worked in fine thread if so wished. The feature of Cluny is its leaves and open fan. To achieve this effect, when working the patterns for the leaves, the workers are twisted once before working through the last pair of passives, which are also twisted once between each row. The following two patterns are typical of Cluny.

Pattern 5 (Fig. 4.13)
20 bobbins. No. 20 or 40 crochet cotton.

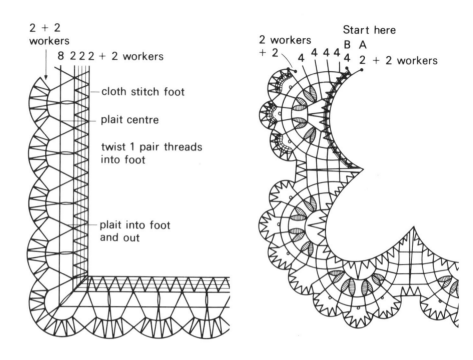

2 + 2
workers

8 2 2 2 + 2 workers

—cloth stitch foot

—plait centre

—twist 1 pair threads
into foot

—plait into foot
and out

Start here
2 workers   B A
+ 2   4 4 4 4   4 2 + 2 workers

Left to right
Figures 4.13 & 14

Pattern 6 (Fig. 4.14)
28 bobbins. No. 20 crochet cotton.

TORCHON LACE

Torchon when translated from the French means 'dish-cloth'. I hope this will
not deter you from making this lace as it has a distinctive characteristic of its
own, being worked at an angle. It is important to remember never to attempt
to work torchon straight across a row or 'up-hill'.

Pattern 7 (Fig. 4.15)
20 bobbins. No. 20 crochet cotton.

Figure 4.15

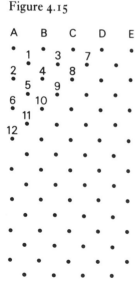

Hang two pairs of bobbins at A, B, C, D and E; twist second and third pairs,
cross, pin up at 1, twist and cross once again.

The following abbreviations will be used:

t. twist   c. cross   p. pin

t.c. 1 and 2, p. up at 2

t.c., t.c. 4 and 5, p. up at 3

t.c., t.c. 3 and 4, p. up at 4

t.c., t.c. 2 and 3, p. up at 5

t.c., t.c. 1 and 2, p. up at 6

t.c., t.c. 6 and 7, p. up at 7

t.c., t.c. 5 and 6, p. up at 8

t.c., t.c. 4 and 5, p. up at 9

t.c., t.c. 3 and 4, p. up at 10

t.c., t.c. 2 and 3, p. up at 11

t.c., t.c. 1 and 2, p. up at 12

t.c., Continue pattern in same manner
following numbers on diagram.
You will find this a very quick
mesh to make.

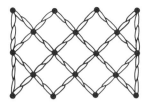

Pattern 7 (Fig. 4.16) Dieppe net ground
20 bobbins. No. 20 crochet cotton.
This is worked exactly the same as Torchon but has two twists.

Pattern 7 (Fig. 4.17) Net
20 bobbins. No. 20 crochet cotton.
Again the same pricking as before, but twist three times between crossings.
The pin is left uncovered.

Pattern 7 (Fig. 4.18) Brussels
20 bobbins. No. 20 crochet cotton.
This is the same pricking but two twists are made, followed by two plait-stitches. These plait-stitches must also be worked at the edge. Pins should not be necessary but, if used at the top and bottom of the plait, should be removed as soon as possible.

Pattern 8 (Fig. 4.19) Rose net ground
24 bobbins. No. 20 crochet cotton.

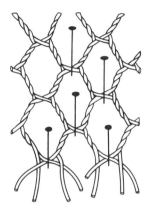

Above
Figures 4.16 & 17
Left to right
Figures 4.18 & 19

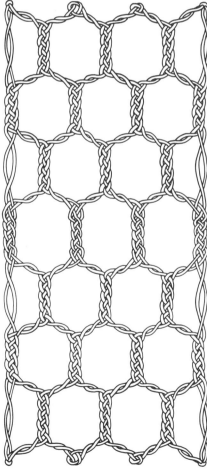

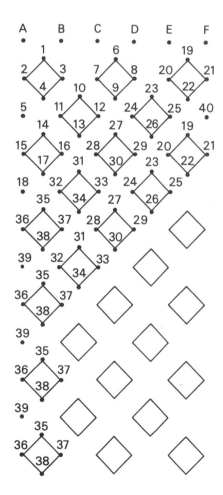

This requires a different technique. Make the following pricking:

Hang two pairs at A, B, C, D, E and F:

t.c. 2nd and 3rd, p. in 1, t.c.; t.c. 1st and 2nd, p. in 2, t.c.; t.c. 3rd and 4th, p. in 3, t.c.; t.c. 2nd and 3rd, p. in 4, t.c.; t.c. 1st and 2nd, p. in 5, t.c.; t.c. 6th and 7th, p. in 6, t.c.; t.c. 5th and 6th, p. in 7, t.c.; t.c. 7th and 8th, p. in 8, t.c.; t.c. 6th and 7th, p. in 9, t.c.; t.c. 5th and 6th, t.c. 3rd and 4th, t.c. 4th and 5th, p. in 10, t.c.; t.c. 3rd and 4th, p. in 11, t.c.; t.c. 5th and 6th, p. in 12, t.c.; t.c. 4th and 5th, p. in 13, t.c.; t.c. 3rd and 4th, t.c. 2nd and 3rd, p. in 14, t.c.; t.c. 1st and 2nd, p. in 15, t.c.; t.c. 3rd and 4th, p. in 16, t.c.; t.c. 2nd and 3rd, p. in 17, t.c.; t.c. 1st and 2nd, p. in 18, t.c.

* t.c. 10th and 11th, p. in 19, t.c.; t.c. 9th and 10th, p. in 20, t.c.; t.c. 11th and 12th, p. in 21, t.c.; t.c. 10th and 11th, p. in 22, t.c.; t.c. 9th and 10th, t.c. 7th and 8th, t.c. 8th and 9th, p. in 23, t.c.; t.c. 7th and 8th, p. in 24, t.c.; t.c. 9th and 10th, p. in 25, t.c.; t.c. 8th and 9th, p. in 26, t.c.; t.c. 7th and 8th, t.c. 5th and 6th, t.c. 6th and 7th, p. in 27, t.c.; t.c. 5th and 6th, p. in 28, t.c.; t.c. 7th and 8th, p. in 29, t.c.; t.c. 6th and 7th, p. in 30, t.c.; t.c. 5th and 6th, t.c. 3rd and 4th, t.c. 4th and 5th, p. in 31, t.c.; t.c. 3rd and 4th, p. in 32, t.c.; t.c. 5th and 6th, p. in 33, t.c.; t.c. 4th and 5th, p. in 34, t.c.; t.c. 3rd and 4th, t.c. 2nd and 3rd, p. in 35, t.c.; t.c. 1st and 2nd, p. in 36, t.c.; t.c. 3rd and 4th, p. in 37, t.c.; t.c. 2nd and 3rd, p. in 38, t.c.; t.c. 1st and 2nd, p. in 39, t.c.; t.c. 11th and 12th, p. in 40, t.c.; t.c. 9th and 10th.

Repeat from *.

I have written these instructions out in detail as so many students find this ground difficult on their first attempt. There are many variations of Rose Net Ground (See *Manual of Bobbin Lace Work* by Margaret Maidment).

Figure 4.20

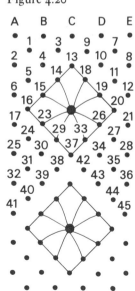

Pattern 9 (Fig. 4.20) Torchon with spiders

20 bobbins. No. 20 crochet cotton.

Hang four bobbins at A, B, C, D and E.

Work Torchon until 19, twist the pairs from 14, 15, 18, 19, three times. Now pass 14 and 15 through 18 and 19 in whole-stitch and pin up in centre. You will now have two pairs of bobbins either side of the pin. Gently pull into position, work whole-stitch from outside to centre, whole-stitch centre pairs. The bobbins will now have returned to their original side, twist pairs three times, return to torchon background.

Pattern 10 (Fig. 4.21) Torchon with blocks

Continue in torchon, work blocks as follows:

Take pin from 6 and 9. Spread out as for a leaf. Weave until the block has been completed.

Pattern 11 (Fig. 4.22) Torchon with leaves

These are worked in the same manner. At the end of the leaf, pin up at B, make a whole-stitch, return pairs to background. The following patterns are all in the torchon family.

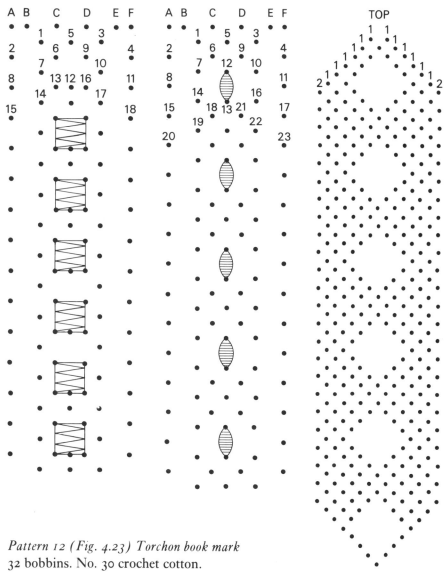

Left to right
Figures 4.21–23
Below
Figure 4.24

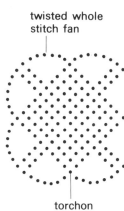

twisted whole
stitch fan

torchon
centre

Left to right
Figures 4.21–23
Below
Figure 4.24

Pattern 12 (Fig. 4.23) Torchon book mark
32 bobbins. No. 30 crochet cotton.

Pattern 13 (Fig. 4.24) Torchon motif
22 bobbins. No. 40 crochet cotton.

RUSSIAN BRAID LACE

This lace is worked in braid, which forms the whole pattern and requires small numbers of bobbins. It is especially suitable for the beginner. It can be made in thick or fine thread, both of which produce effective lace, and may be plain (Fig. 4.25) or waved (Fig. 4.26). It is suitable for table or personal linen.

Pattern 14 (Fig. 4.25) Plain braid
12 bobbins. No. 20 crochet cotton.
Pin up four bobbins at A, four at B and two at C. Commence at A. Make a

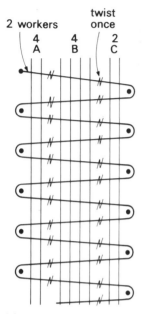

2 workers | twist once

4 A | 4 B | 2 C

Figure 4.25

whole-stitch, pin up two pairs behind pin. With inner pair make one twist. Work whole-stitch through four passives, twist worker once, whole-stitch through last passive pair, pin up two pairs of bobbins behind pin using inner pair one twist. Whole-stitch back across four passive bobbins, twist workers once, whole-stitch through last pair of passives, pin up. Repeat until required length has been made.

Pattern 15 (Fig. 4.26) Waved braid
14 bobbins. No. 20 crochet cotton.
Pin up four bobbins at A, six at B, two at C, using the same method as for plain braid. Work until 5 has been reached. Work across the eight passive bobbins, twist workers once and pin up at 6. Return back across the eight passive bobbins leaving end pair unworked. This is called working a blind pin. Repeat at 8 and 10. At 12 twist unworked bobbins three times, work whole-stitch through, pin up as usual. This will form the curve in the braid and will be worked either side.

MAKING CORNERS

As you become more experienced you may come across patterns which do not have a corner or you may wish to redesign the original corner. This is not difficult. You will need a small flat mirror, sticky tape and either a photocopy of the pattern or a tracing.

Place the mirror across the lace pattern, move the mirror around to an angle of 45° when you will see the corner formed in the mirror. Draw a line along the edge of the mirror (Fig. 4.27).

Cut the pattern along this line. Place pattern at corner angle and stick down with tape. You now have a corner. You may have to add extra bobbins to work the corner.

Left to right
Figures 4.26 & 27

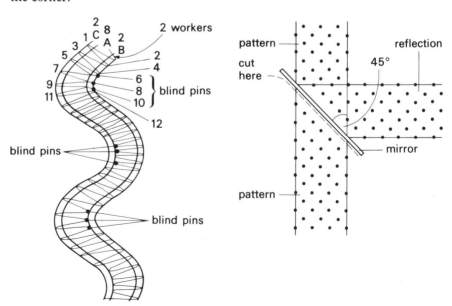

46

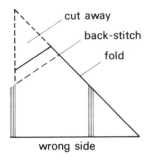

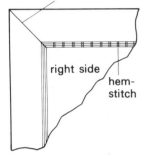

Figure 4.28

Figure 4.29

MOUNTING OF LACE

When you have made your lace, great care must be taken when mounting it. Bad mounting will ruin any good work you have done. I have seen many beautiful pieces of lace ruined because of untidy mounting.

Prepare some linen as follows for hem-stitching:

Measure the lace carefully, and cut the linen to size, allowing a hem turning. Pull two or three threads, depending on the fineness of the linen. Hem-stitch along the hem.

To mitre a corner (Fig. 4.28) fold the hem over to where the threads have been pulled, using either threads pulled from linen or the thread used to make the lace, if it is a fine thread, and a tapestry-needle. Lace may be attached to linen using any of the following methods.

Whipping stitch Place the lace on to the linen and tack it into position. Oversew the lace to the linen. Carefully cut away any surplus linen from the back of the work. Roll a very small hem and secure it with plain hem-stitch.

Punch- or pin-stitch Place the lace on the linen and tack it into position. With a tapestry-needle and suitable thread, working from right to left, make two back-stitches through the lace and linen from 1 to 2 and bring the needle across the work to 3. This will be on linen only. Two back-stitches are made between 3 and 4; take the needle across the back of the work and out at 1; one back-stitch is made between 1 and 5. Proceed along the hem using this sequence. You will have a square-stitch on the front of the work and a cross-stitch on the back. This is especially suitable for scalloped lace (see Fig. 4.29).

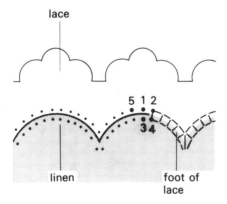

Button-hole mounting Place lace as described in Punch-stitch method. Work from left to right making very small button-hole-stitches. Finish off the back as for whipping-stitch.

Care of lace

Many a beautiful piece of lace has been ruined because of bad laundering or storage.

LAUNDERING

Always use pure soap flakes, never detergent or bleach. Using hand-warm water, gently place lace in suds—do *not* squeeze or rub. Leave lace to soak for a few minutes, gently moving it around in the bowl. When clean, rinse thoroughly in warm water. Never hang lace up to dry. Have ready a board, well padded with a thick towel and covered with a piece of white sheeting. Place lace on the board, gently pull into shape and pin out any picots. Leave to dry but not in contact with direct heat, e.g. direct sunlight, radiators, gas or electric fires; never iron dry.

Narrow lace may be laundered in the following way:
Using a large bottle, preferably quart-sized, wrap a piece of white calico or sheeting around the bottle until it is well padded. Sew a seam to secure it. Wrap the lace around the bottle—tack the end to secure. Place the 'lace bottle' in a bucket of warm suds and soak for 1 hour, or longer if the lace is heavily soiled. Rotate the bottle occasionally. If the lace remains soiled, prepare more suds in a large pan and boil the 'lace bottle' for 20 minutes. Remove the lace bottle and rinse in warm water. Repeat the rinsing until the water is clear. Place it on a clean towel and pat out the surplus water. Leave it in a warm place to dry, but again not in direct heat. Remove the lace when it is dry. It should not need ironing.

STIFFENING

The lace should be laundered and quite dry. Make starch as follows: mix 1 tablespoon of starch with 2 tablespoons of *cold* water. Add 0.56 l (1 pt) of boiling water. The starch will thicken. Dilute it with 1.1 l (2 pt) of cold water to make a medium starch. Dab or spray the starch over the pinned-out lace or plunge the lace bottle into the starch. 'Beat' the starch into the lace by slapping the lace with the palm of the hand. Take care when carrying out this process on fine lace. Leave it to dry. *Never* use a spray-on starch.

IRONING MOUNTED LACE

Iron when the linen is slightly damp. Place the lace on a well padded ironing-board, cover with a clean cloth and iron. Take care not to have the iron too hot.

TINTING LACE

Add colouring to starch. A little strong coffee will produce a cream-coloured lace, strong tea (cold) will produce a light beige. When tinting lace, experiment on an old piece first.

STORING LACE

No lace should be stored for any length of time with starch in it as the starch will cause cracks in folded fabrics.

Lace should never be stored folded. Tablecloths, trolley cloths, large tray cloths, all should be laid between sheets of blue tissue and rolled on to a cardboard roll (these can be obtained at any fabric shop). Finally wrap in a piece of sheeting. It is quite a good idea to list the contents of each roll. Handkerchiefs should be stored flat.

Baby-gowns and dresses (this includes women's dresses) are better hung from well padded hangers in a suitable cupboard and hung out in the fresh air at least every 6 months. It is advisable to launder or dry-clean dresses at least once a year.

Dried lavender or tansy sprinkled between layers of lace (remember to hang a bag in with dresses) will keep moths at bay. Do not use any chemicals.

Sample books

Students very often feel it is a waste of time keeping a sample book but it will prove a useful reference. A loose-leaf folder is ideal. Make your samples and mount them on dark blue or black card. Label and slip them into a polythene sleeve. Keep a notebook and write in any new technique; also keep a list of suppliers.

Further information

MUSEUMS

Once you have started to make lace you will probably wish to visit museums and look at collections. If you do, it is advisable to write to the museum curator first, asking if there is a reserve collection (some museums do have one). Ask if you may see it, stating any preference. Also ask if there are any patterns available of which you may take rubbings (using wax stick and tracing paper), or if photocopies are available.

The following museums are well worth visiting:

Luton Museum, Wardown Park, Luton Bedfordshire. Specialists in Bedfordshire lace, lace-making equipment and bobbins. The very helpful assistant curator, Mrs Fudge, will cope with parties from one to fifty.

Salisbury Museum, Salisbury, Wiltshire. Over two hundred samples of Downton lace. No patterns available at the moment. Small parties only.

Bucks County Museum, Aylesbury, Buckinghamshire. Buckinghamshire lace; patterns available.

Exeter Museum, Exeter, Devon. Honiton lace; patterns available. Large reserve collection.

Victoria and Albert Museum, Exhibition Road, London, SW7. Continental and English lace. The department cannot take large parties into the reserve collection.

There are some private collections listed in the Guild of Lace Register.

SUPPLIERS

These are now more plentiful.

Mrs Audrey Sells, Lane Cove, 49 Pedley Lane, Cliffton, Shefford, Bedfordshire, U.K.

Braggins, 26/36 Silver Street, Bedford, Bedfordshire, U.K.

LACE SOCIETIES

Guild of Lace: Membership Secretary, Mrs C. Berrow, 7 Southwood Close, Kingswinford, W. Midlands, U.K.

International Old Lacers of America: English Director, M/s J. Pegg, 90 Kimberley Rd, Southborne, Bournemouth, Dorset, U.K.

Nottinghamshire Bobbin Lace Society: Mrs J. C. Saunders, 29 Patterdale Road, Woodthorpe, Nottingham, U.K.

PEGGY TUCK AND PATRICIA LACEY

5 Traditional English Smocking

TRADITIONAL ENGLISH hand-smocking, as it is seen today, is identical to the beautiful handiwork created by nineteenth-century country-women in adorning their menfolk's smocks. Yet the art of smocking evolved over many centuries for purely practical reasons. Quite simply, smocking is a method of controlling fullness by using ornamental embroidery to hold in place a series of gathered pleats.

From Norman times in Britain, the smock was an undergarment worn by both sexes. Where it was seen, at the neck and wrists, it was invariably decorated with some sort of needlework. As time went on, fashion decreed that the neck of the overdress be cut down to display the fine stitching on the smock.

Throughout the centuries, examples of stitches looking remarkably similar to present-day smocking can be seen on the clothes of the upper classes in portraits. But it was only when the country-folk adopted the smock or smock-frock in the late eighteenth century, and women rivalled each other in lavish ornamentation, that smocking as such became recognised.

The English smock, considered by many to be *the* national folk costume of the country, was worn for over a century. A loose garment, of strong, hand-woven linen, the smock incorporated the same stitches as those used today to gather in the extra fullness at the yoke and on the sleeves, complemented by lavish embroidery, mostly in feather-stitch, decorating the collar, yoke and sides of the smock. Most of the embroidery designs symbolised the occupation of the wearer.

The colour of the workaday smocks, usually quite drab, varied from county to county, but everywhere the best, or Sunday, smock was white with white smocking and embroidery. Many good examples of traditional smocks are preserved in museums throughout Britain.

From the late nineteenth century, smocking was seen as a decoration for children's and ladies' clothing. Although babies' and little girls' hand-smocked dresses have been in vogue ever since, adult fashion periodically restores smocking to a high place in the fashion world, whether, as recently, in a revival of the folk smock and peasant blouse, or as decoration on dresses and even winter coats. To cope with the demand for smocked garments, manufacturers have tried to create the look of smocking with machines; but nothing can compare with the beauty and natural elasticity of traditional English hand-smocking.

Materials and equipment

suitable materials for smocking	pins
paper dress-making patterns	needles
transfer dotted paper	scissors
good quality stranded embroidery thread	tape measure
	coloured pencils
reels of strong cotton thread	

CHOICE OF FABRIC

Traditional smocks were so durable that they lasted from generation to generation. Today's smocking can also last, provided that good quality materials and embroidery threads are used. Considering the time and effort that goes into hand-smocking, it would be sad to see it wasted on poor quality materials that do not wear well.

The linen used for the original smocks was heavy and coarse and difficult to work with. Today's smocker is fortunate to have a wide range of fabrics to choose from. Most fabrics can be smocked, but for the best results and ease of working choose a fabric that is washable, soft to the touch and with good draping qualities. Cottons and cotton/man-made fibre mixtures are good for summer wear and woollen/cotton mixtures for warmer winter clothes. Gingham is particularly useful since the preparation of the fabric for smocking is easier and the checks provide a good straight line guide to follow when actually smocking. Each fabric is different and only experience will teach the smocker at a touch which are the best to work with.

Paper dress-making patterns for smocked clothes are available, but other patterns can be adapted, providing sufficient extra material is allowed for the smocking. Generally three times the finished width must be allowed, e.g. material 0.9m (36in) wide will smock down to 30cm (12in). This general rule varies according to the individual tension of the smocker, the stitches worked (some smock the material more tightly than others), and the fabric itself: more of a thin, fine material will be required for smocking than of a thicker, coarser fabric. It is essential to try a test sample to check the tension before starting work and risking disappointment.

THREAD

For smocking, good quality stranded embroidery thread must be used. Generally, three strands are sufficient to show up the work clearly, but again this does depend on the fabric used: a very fine fabric may need only two strands, while a heavier winter fabric may take four, or even six, strands. A good guide to the overall effect is the sample piece, held at arm's length. If the smocking does not stand out, working with an extra strand of thread may help.

Basic techniques

PREPARATION OF FABRIC

Smocking is very time-consuming and much time must be spent beforehand in the tedious preparation of the material before one decorative stitch is sewn. It is frustrating to have to spend several hours on the initial pleating of the material when you long to see the colourful smocking, but it cannot be stressed too strongly that the final effect of the smocking does depend to a very large extent on careful preparation. Even experienced smockers must ensure that the material is gathered accurately, with uniform pleats on which the design can be worked and which will provide the proper elasticity when the garment is finished.

The material must be gathered into regular, even pleats and the simplest way to do this is with smocking transfers of dots. The dotted paper is available from needlework shops in various spacings for use on different thicknesses of material. Your shop will advise the best width-spacing for your particular material. A fine fabric needs dots close together to make smaller pleats, while a thicker fabric will need dots further apart to give deeper pleats.

The dots must always be placed onto the *wrong* side of the fabric so that they do not show when the work is finished. Tack the paper onto the wrong side, to make sure it does not slip, and press with an iron (set at the correct heat-setting for the fabric) to print the dots onto the material. Always test a small piece of material first to ensure, on a fine coloured fabric, that the dots do not show through to the right side and, on a dark or printed fabric, that you can see them. The transfer dotted paper is available in two colours, blue and yellow, to suit most fabrics.

On some very fine fabrics and some multi-colour prints, it will not be possible to transfer the dots by iron and it will be necessary to tack the paper onto the wrong side of the material and sew each dot as described below through the paper and the material, tearing away the paper when complete to leave no trace of dots.

Use as many rows of dots as you need for the depth of smocking required, although it is sometimes useful to allow one extra row at the top of the work to use as a straight guide when sewing the smocked section into the garment you are making. In this case, the top row of gathering-threads must be left in place when the others are removed.

Figure 5.1

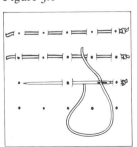

To gather the material, first thread a sewing-needle with strong sewing-thread, longer than the width of the material and sufficiently vivid in colour to be seen clearly on the material. Tie a big knot in the end of the thread and insert the needle at the first row on the right-hand side of the material.

Working from right to left, pick up each dot along the row, putting the needle into the fabric on the right-hand side of the first dot and bringing it up on the left side of the same dot (Fig. 5.1). Run the thread through to the next dot, insert the needle on one side and out through the other side of the same dot. Repeat to the end of the row. Remove the needle and leave the spare thread

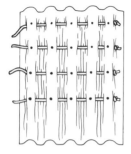

Figure 5.2

loose at the end of the row. Follow the same procedure for each row of dots taking care to align the stitches.

When all the rows of dots have been tacked, the threads must be pulled up carefully, a few rows at a time, to pleat the material to a width an inch or so smaller than the finished smocking width required (Fig. 5.2). Each thread should be tied firmly at the loose end to prevent the gathers slipping. Turn the material over and you are ready to begin smocking.

STITCHES

An elaborate piece of smocking may look very complicated, but don't be alarmed! Most smocking is merely a variation of the basic outline- or rope-stitch. Once mastered, this stitch and its variations can be used together to create an infinite range of designs.

In smocking, the pleats are held together and the elasticity obtained by embroidering the stitches over the pleats. For each stitch, the needle must be inserted to pick up the top half of each pleat and the thread pulled up to close the pleats together, then carried onto the next stitch. The thread must never be pulled too tightly or the work will be uneven and the colour will not be seen. Nor must the thread be left too slack, or the pleats will not be held firmly enough together and the work will be too loose and will not fit.

It is vital to work a test piece to check (and if necessary correct) tension and the amount of material needed for individual stitches. This will avoid wasting good material and the consequent disappointment of a garment that does not fit.

To start smocking, thread a needle with the required number of strands of embroidery thread and tie a knot in the end. The thread should be long enough to complete each row to avoid unnecessary joins. Obviously some rows with a larger number of stitches (e.g. diamond- or wave-stitch) will take more thread than the initial outline-stitch, but a good guide to the amount of thread required is three times the width of the pleated material. The length can be adjusted on following rows.

If you do run out of thread in the middle or near the end of a row, fasten off the first thread firmly with several stitches on a pleat at the back of the work. To join in the new thread, again use several small stitches on the back of the work (a knot may pull through when the smocking is stretched in wear) and bring the thread through to the right side of the work at the correct point to continue the pattern. Remember to allow more thread on following rows to avoid running out again.

All stitches except Vandyke are worked from left to right and a piece of smocking is invariably started with at least one row of outline- (rope-) or cable-stitch to hold the pleats more firmly. The position of the thread above or below the needle is vital for the correct working of each stitch. The thread must always be kept *above* the needle when working stitches down and *below* the needle when working stitches up.

54

Outline or rope-stitch (Fig. 5.3) Working from left to right, bring the needle up from the back of the work to the left side of pleat 1. Keeping the thread above the needle and slanting the needle down, pick up the top half of pleat 2 to the right. Pull the thread through and draw the pleats together. Keeping the thread above the needle and the needle slanting down, pick up pleat 3 to the right and continue to pick up each pleat in this way to the end of the row. Take the needle through to the back of the work and fasten off firmly.

To keep the line of stitches straight, it is simplest to work this stitch along a row of gathering-stitches, using the gathering-thread as a guide.

For a different effect when working outline-stitch, keep the thread below the needle and the needle pointed up. This reverses the direction of the stitch. Two rows of outline-stitch worked in opposite directions produce an arrow-head design.

Left to right
Figures 5.3 & 4

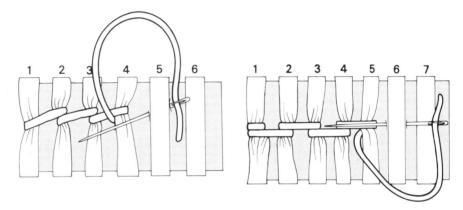

Cable-stitch (Fig. 5.4) This is worked in the same way as outline-stitch, straight along a row of gathering-thread, but for cable the thread is held alternately above and below the needle and the needle is always in a horizontal position.

Working from left to right, bring the needle up from the back of the work to the left side of pleat 1. With the thread above the needle and the needle horizontal, pick up the top half of pleat 2 to the right and draw the two pleats together. For the next stitch, keep the thread below the needle but keep the needle horizontal and pick up pleat 3. Continue to the end of the row, picking up each pleat to the right but holding the thread alternately above and below the needle. Fasten off firmly on the wrong side of the work.

Double Cable-stitch (Fig. 5.5) Work one row as above and, for the second row, start the first stitch with the thread below the needle, the second stitch with the thread above the needle and continue alternating the position of the thread to reverse the pattern.

Wave-stitch (Fig. 5.6) This stitch is worked diagonally between the rows of gathering-thread over a number of pleats. Working from left to right, bring the needle up from the back of the work to the left of pleat 1. With the needle

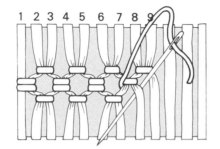 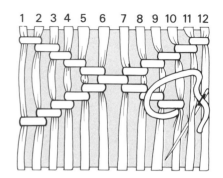

Left to right
Figures 5.5 & 6

in a horizontal position and the thread below the needle, pick up the top half of pleat 2 and draw together. To work up the wave, keep the thread below the needle and slant the needle slightly upwards. Pick up pleat 3, slightly above the previous stitch, and draw the pleats together. Keeping the thread below the needle and the needle slanting slightly up, repeat with pleats 4 and 5. Place the thread above the needle, keep the needle horizontal and pick up pleat 6 level with pleat 5. To work down the wave, keep the thread above the needle, slant the needle slightly down and pick up pleat 7 level with pleat 4, pleat 8 level with pleat 3, pleat 9 level with pleat 2. For the straight-stitch at the base of the wave, put the thread below the needle, keep the needle horizontal and pick up pleat 10 level with pleat 9. The wave is now complete and should be repeated along the whole row. Fasten the thread off firmly on the back of the work.

For a smaller wave, reduce the number of stitches rising before levelling the wave and coming down, thus using fewer pleats.

Wave-stitch is used in single rows or over several rows in the same or different colours worked closely together. By reversing the direction of the wave (work first down, then up) on subsequent rows a trellis-shape can be effected.

The main rule to remember when working a wave or trellis is, whenever working stitches up, keep the thread below the needle and the needle slanting up; whenever working stitches down, keep the thread above the needle and the needle slanting down. Always keep the stitches level with the corresponding stitch on the other side of the wave.

Diamond-stitch (Fig. 5.7) Diamond-stitch is worked between two rows of gathering-threads, with the direction of the stitches reversing on alternate rows to complete the diamond-shape.

Working from left to right, bring the needle up from the back of the work to the left side of pleat 1, half-way between two rows of gathering threads. With the needle horizontal and the thread below the needle, pick up the top half of pleat 2 and draw the pleats together. With the needle horizontal and the thread below the needle, pick up pleat 3, level with the upper gathering-thread and draw together. Put the thread above the needle, again horizontal, pick up pleat 4 level with pleat 3 and draw together. Keep the thread above the needle

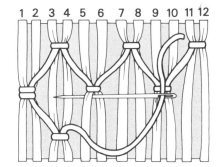 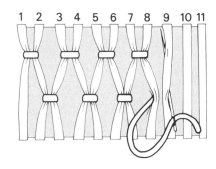

Left to right
Figures 5.7 & 8

and the needle horizontal, pick up pleat 5 level with pleat 2 and draw together. Now bring the thread below the needle, still horizontal, and pick up pleat 6 level with pleat 5 and draw together. Continue working the stitches up and down in this way to the end of the row. Fasten off firmly on a pleat at the back of the work.

On the second row, work the stitches down, then up, to complete the diamond. For a block of diamonds, work the third row as the first, the fourth as the second and so on until the desired depth is reached.

Honeycomb-stitch (Fig. 5.8) This is the most elastic of all smocking stitches and is best worked alone rather than combined with other stitches. Working from left to right, bring the needle through from the back of the work to the top of pleat 1 level with a row of gathering-thread. With the thread above the needle and the needle horizontal, stitch through the top of pleats 2 and 1 and draw together. Sew them with a second stitch, but this time take the needle down the centre of pleat 2 at the back of the work to the second row of gathering-thread. Bring the needle through to the front of the work and catch together pleats 3 and 2. Sew with a second stitch, this time taking the needle up through the back of pleat 3 to come out at the front of the work level with the first row of gathering-thread. Continue working up and down, keeping the long threads behind the work to the end of the row. Fasten off firmly at the back of the work.

The second row of honeycomb is worked between the third and fourth rows of gathering-threads.

Surface Honeycomb-stitch (Fig. 5.9) This is also a very elastic stitch and when worked gives the appearance of a small diamond. It is worked in a similar way to honeycomb-stitch, but the long threads are kept visible on the right side of the work.

Working from left to right along a row of gathering-thread, bring the needle through from the back of the work to the left of pleat 1. Holding the needle horizontally and the thread above the needle, pick up the top half of pleat 2 and draw together. Leave the thread above the needle and insert the needle in the right-hand side of pleat 2, half-way between the rows of gathering-thread,

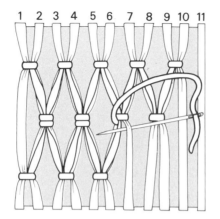
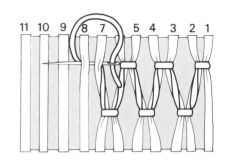

Left to right
Figures 5.9 & 10

and draw it through. Place the thread below the needle, still horizontal, pick up pleat 3 and draw together. The next stitch returns to the upper row of gathering-thread. With the thread below the needle, insert the needle on the right-hand side of pleat 3 and pull the thread through. With the thread above the needle, pick up pleat 4 and draw together. Continue picking up each pleat in this manner, always remembering to keep the thread above the needle when working down and the thread below the needle when working up. Fasten the thread off firmly at the back of the work.

For the second row, to complete the diamond-shape, bring the needle from the back of the work to the left side of pleat 1 level with the lower row of gathering-thread. With the thread below the needle, pick up pleat 2 along the gathering-line and draw together. Keeping the thread below the needle, pick up pleat 2 half-way between the rows of gathering-thread to meet the lower stitch of the first row. With the thread above the needle, pick up pleat 3 and draw together. With the thread above the needle again, return the needle to the lower row of gathering-thread and pick up pleat 3. Pull the thread through, put the thread below the needle, pick up pleat 4 and draw together. Continue in this way, picking up each pleat to complete diamond-shapes along the row.

Vandyke stitch (Fig. 5.10) Unlike other stitches, this stitch is worked from *right* to *left*. Bring the needle up from the back of the work to the left side of pleat 2. With the thread above the needle, make a stitch across pleats 1 and 2 and draw together. With the thread above the needle, take the needle down the right side of pleat 2 to the required depth for the stitch, pass the needle through pleats 2 and 3 and pull through. Now put the thread below the needle, make a stitch across pleats 2 and 3 and draw together. With the thread below the needle, take the needle up and pick up pleats 3 and 4. Pull the thread through. With the thread above the needle, make a stitch across pleats 3 and 4 and draw together. With the thread above the needle, take the needle down and pick up pleats 4 and 5. Pull the thread through. With the thread below the needle, make a stitch across pleats 4 and 5. Continue up and down in this way to the end of the row and fasten off firmly at the back of the work.

58

1 Ropecraft. A selection of items made from various knots.

2 Macramé. Plant pot hanger.

3 Crochet. Matinée jacket and hairpin-crocheted table centre.

4 Tatting. Edgings and motifs.

5 Bobbin lace. Lace in the making and examples of patterns.

6 Traditional English smocking. Child's dress, doll's dress and lally bag.

7 Samplers and stitchery. Use of gold thread, cords, beads and applied padded leather and snakeskin.

8 Samplers and stitchery. Sampler of Cretan stitches worked in various threads.

9 Quilting. Sample of machine quilting.

10 Quilting. Evening jacket showing wadded quilting.

11 Patchwork. Bedspread made from scraps of silk ties, begun in 1870.

12 Patchwork. Box decorated with design of hexagons.

13 Pressed flowers. Book mark, cards, finger plate and gift tags.

14 Pressed flowers. Framed picture.

15 Dorset buttons. Blandford Cartwheel showing method of joining.

16 Dorset buttons. A selection of old and modern.

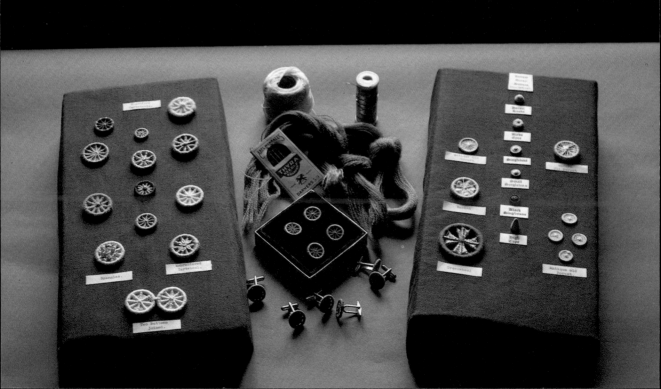

17 Candles. A varied assortment of hand-made moulded and embossed candles.

18 Puppetry. Pop-up puppet concealed in pot.

19 Puppetry. Pop-up puppet popping out of pot.

20 Puppetry. Chicken hand-puppet.

SMOCKING DESIGNS

Before starting work, it is always best to design the overall pattern of your smocking. It is important to consider carefully the colour and general look of the finished work. Count the number of pleats and gathering-rows in the material to be smocked and mark these on plain or graph paper. Consider whether you want a simple design, such as an overall diamond, or if you want a more complicated design using a variety of stitches and colours.

Using coloured pencils, draw a picture of the smocking design you would like to see, using straight lines for the outline- or cable-stitches and ups and downs for the waves or diamonds. In this way you will get an idea of the effect of the combination of colours and shapes that can be achieved. Fig. 5.11 shows a sample of finished smocking based on a simple two-colour design on paper.

The basic rules to be observed in designing smocking are to achieve a good balance of shape and colour. The first line of smocking is invariably done in outline- or cable-stitch, since this provides a firm anchorage for the rest of the smocking. Counting the number of pleats is important to ensure balance in the overall pattern. For example, one point of a small diamond takes four

Figure 5.11

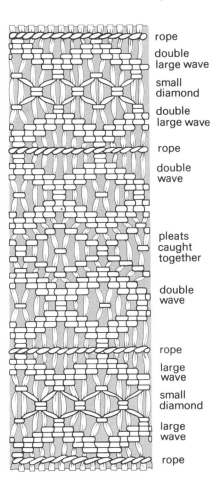

rope
double
large wave

small
diamond

double
large wave

rope

double
wave

pleats
caught
together

double
wave

rope

large
wave

small
diamond

large
wave

rope

pleats but you must allow an extra pleat at each end of the row for the securing stitch; the wave-stitch takes an even number of pleats, plus an extra pleat at each end of the row. When planning a large pattern, such as a wave or trellis, ensure that the centre of a wave comes to the centre of the work.

Spacing of rows is all important. Small spaces between rows enhance the stitching, but do avoid large gaps since, with repeated wear and washing, the pleats which are not held firmly with stitches will pop open and spoil the effect of the smocking. To a certain extent this can be overcome by pulling the pleats into position from top to bottom after washing, but it is far better simply to avoid the problem.

This problem can also be met when working large diamonds, but this can be overcome, and you can add to the attractiveness of the pattern, by working a French knot or simply oversewing two or three stitches across the two centre pleats of the diamond (Fig. 5.11). The thread can be cut for each centre knot or it can be run loosely across the back of the work to the next diamond.

Choosing the colours for smocking is basically a matter of personal taste. When using plain fabrics, smocking can be most effective in a single colour, either toning or as a complete contrast. With a dark fabric, a vivid shade can be enhanced with discreet use of white or cream; a pale fabric is usually most attractive smocked in one bold colour only or in a bold colour plus a toning shade one shade deeper than the fabric.

When using a patterned material, it is always best to choose one of the pre-dominant colours in a brighter shade to tone with the print. Where multi-colour smocking is wanted, choose from the other shades in the print. Try to avoid contrasting colours on prints. To make the smocking more noticeable on prints, it is often advisable to use an extra strand of embroidery thread.

FINISHING THE WORK

Having completed the smocking, and before taking out the gathering-threads, the work must be steamed on the wrong side. This will set the pleats firmly in place and make the smocking stitches stand out more on the front.

To do this, pin the smocking right side down onto an ironing-board to keep the material flat. Place a damp cloth over the pleats and pass the iron gently over the cloth. Be careful not to let the weight of the iron actually press the work because this would merely flatten it. Remove the damp cloth and let the work dry naturally before unpinning and removing the gathering-threads.

When laundering smocked garments, *never press or iron the smocking*. Once the gathering-threads have been removed, ironing the smocking will not only flatten the work but will press out the pleats, removing all elasticity and loosening the smocked section.

When sewing smocked material into the yoke of a garment, it is best to line the yoke and insert the raw edge at the top of the smocking between the yoke and lining. This gives a firmer hold to the smocked material as well as giving a neater finish.

Where smocking extends to the side, underarm or sleeve seams, catch the first and last stitches in each row into the seam to give a firmer hold.

If smocking is to be inset for purely decorative reasons and no elasticity is needed, the smocking should first be completely lined.

Uses of smocking

There are many uses for smocking. Perhaps the more familiar are for children's clothing, whether baby-dresses and rompers with a few rows of smocking around the neck or beneath a yoke, or a small girl's more elaborate dress smocked to the waist.

The natural elasticity of smocking makes it an ideal alternative to elastic or a separate cuff to hold in the fullness of sleeves at the wrist, whether for children's or adults' clothes.

Smocking can also be used to replace ordinary gathering on women's clothing. This is particularly attractive on nightdresses, under a yoke on bedjackets, blouses or loose full dresses. Where the decoration of smocking is wanted, but not necessarily the maximum fullness which would result, an inset piece of smocking would be the answer. This should always be lined. A lined inset could be used for smocked pockets on a dress or apron, or a smocked inset yoke on a dress, kaftan or nightdress.

The waistband of a dirndl skirt can be smocked, but it must be remembered that this will stretch with wear and it is, therefore, advisable to line the back of the smocking to the required waist size and fasten the skirt as normal with a zip or side placket.

Apart from practice samplers to try different smocking-stitches, the new smocker will find great satisfaction in making a simple, small item before starting on a larger project.

Projects

LALLY BAG

To make a simple smocked lally bag (Pl. 6), take a piece of material measuring 60 cm (24 in) by 23 cm (9 in). Make a narrow hem along the top (long) edge and transfer four rows of gathering-dots, the first row 2.5 cm (1 in) below the top edge to leave a frill at the top when finished. Gather the material and draw up the gathers to 18 cm (7 in).

Work a simple smocking design, such as two rows of cable-stitch close together on the first gathering-row, followed by four rows of surface honeycomb, starting mid-way between the first two gathering-rows, and ending with two more rows of cable-stitch close together on the bottom gathering-row. Set the smocking by steaming and remove the gathering-thread.

Fold the material in half and stitch along the side and base, using a French seam to avoid the necessity for lining. Using two pieces of ribbon 23 cm (9 in) long, make two handles and sew inside the bag, one on each side below the frill.

Little girls love these bags, particularly when they match a dress of their own. The size can be varied according to the age of the child. For adults a more elaborate evening-bag, roller-bag or work-bag can also be made using this method.

NIGHTDRESS

An attractive nightdress can be easily and effectively made, even by those without a great deal of dress-making experience. By adjusting the width and length of the material used, this idea can be used for a nightdress or even a sundress, to fit any size from the smallest toddler to adults. Choose a cotton or polyester/cotton mixture fabric, remembering to check the smocking tension with a small sample before starting work. If the material is very fine, allow a width of fabric greater than the usual three times the required finished smocked width, as it will smock up tighter.

To make a nightdress to fit the average-sized woman, measure the length required from directly under the arm to the hem level (either long or short) and add an allowance for the hem. Cut two pieces of fabric this length and 114 cm (45 in) wide. Sew the two lengths together down one side only. Neaten the top by making a narrow hem, shell-edging or sewing on narrow lace.

Leaving 2.5 cm (1 in) at the top for a frill, gather the full width of the material ready for smocking 7.5 cm (3 in) deep (the final gathering-row for the pleats should be 10 cm (4 in) below the top of the garment). Smock along the gathering-rows, starting, as always, with at least one row of cable- or rope-stitch then progressing to diamond-, wave- or trellis-stitch in your own pattern and colour scheme. Make the smocking fairly tight as it may 'give' a little in wear.

'Set' the finished smocking by steaming; then remove the gathering-threads. Sew up the second side seam, matching the rows of smocking as you do so. Cut four shoulder ties 46 cm (18 in) long by 2.5 cm (1 in) wide, either using ribbon or making them from matching fabric. Attach two ties at the front of the night-dress and two at the back, sewing them inside the garment by catching them with small stitches to the back of the smocking pleats. The two front ties should be approximately 18 cm (7 in) apart and the back ones 13 cm (5 in) apart, to prevent them slipping from the shoulders.

To complete the garment, make a hem round the bottom or edge with lace or a matching frill.

DOLL'S DRESS

Another quick item to make to practice smocking is a doll's dress (Pl. 6). Choose your material and, for the front of the dress, cut a piece three times the finished bodice width required, and the length required from the shoulder. Prepare the material to be smocked to a depth from shoulder to waist and smock in a simple small design. No shaping is needed for the front smocking, but, when binding the neck, cover the middle of the top row of smocking to lower the neckline slightly. Make up the dress, catching the first and last stitches of each row of smocking in the sleeve- and side-seams.

Again, little girls love their dolls to be dressed like them, while older teenagers and the not-so-young appreciate a doll in hand-smocked clothes to adorn their bedrooms.

These simple beginnings will give the new smocker the experience and confidence to go on to recreate in more ambitious clothing the beautiful handiwork that has become a traditional English craft.

YVONNE MORTON

6 Samplers and Stitchery

THE SAMPLER, derived from the old French, *exemplaire*, became the pattern book of embroiderers throughout history and the world. There can be no doubt that samplers were made during the Middle Ages but, unfortunately, the earliest surviving ones date from the sixteenth century, when embroidery for domestic use and dress became fashionable.

In the seventeenth century, samplers were worked on narrow strips of linen, sometimes as much as 0.9 m (36 in) in length, rolled up on a small ivory rod and kept by the embroiderer for instant reference. The designs were bold and colourful, with flowers, birds and fish incorporated with the border patterns. Other samplers were worked in cut-work, drawn thread-work and white-work. They were often signed and dated. During the second half of the seventeenth century, it was considered a necessity for young girls to know their needlework and they would, at a very early age, complete a simple stitch sampler before graduating to the more difficult samplers of ornate cut-work patterns and finally to making a box in stump-work, a real achievement.

The eighteenth century saw the sampler change in shape and style by becoming wider and shorter, more like a small panel, with borders of flowers and cross-stitch or tent-stitch motifs scattered around. Poems and biblical texts, quite unsuitable for a young child, were fashionable. Map samplers became popular.

By the nineteenth century, the sampler became more of an exercise in working a variety of alphabets and numerals and, somehow, lost something of the vitality and individuality of earlier work. Samplers became increasingly similar in design and often appeared worked solely in cross-stitch.

During the first half of the twentieth century, Mrs Archibald Christie worked some samplers as they were originally intended—as a record of stitches —and these were photographed and published in her book *Samplers and Stitches* in 1920. Louisa Pesel produced some stitch samplers for the Victoria and Albert Museum, where they can still be seen, which were later published in portfolio form as *Stitches from Old English Embroideries*, *Stitches from Eastern Embroideries* and *Stitches from Western Embroideries*.

Materials and equipment

fabrics	cotton thread
graph paper	needles
plain drawing paper	tapestry-needle
tissue paper	pins
dress-maker's carbon paper	scissors
stranded embroidery cotton	embroidery frame

An even-weave linen, cut carefully to size and oversewn around the edges to prevent fraying, threads such as stranded cottons, which can be separated to make finer threads, and twisted threads, are the requirements, together with a tapestry-needle. An embroidery frame is useful to keep the material taut and aid the counting of the stitches. This can be a ring frame or a slate frame, which is slightly more sophisticated. The slate frame consists of two rollers and two slats which screw together and hold the work which is firmly sewn onto tapes on two sides and laced on the other two sides. This type of frame prevents creasing and soiling the work. Do keep your embroidery clean by keeping the work in an old piece of sheeting or pillowcase while not in use.

Below
Figures 6.1–6

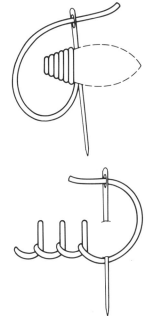

Basic techniques

STITCHES

Stitches can be divided into four main groups; flat, looped, chained and knotted. The most widely practised of flat stitches is *satin-stitch* (Fig. 6.1). A flat stitch pulled out of the straight by another passing across it becomes a loop and examples of these are *blanket-stitch* (Fig. 6.2) and *feather-stitch* (Fig. 6.3). A complete loop becomes a chain-stitch (Fig. 6.4) of which there are many varieties. A *chain-stitch* tightly twisted develops into a knot, such as the *french knot* (Fig. 6.5) and *bullion knot* (Fig. 6.6).

Composite stitches consist of one stitch making the foundation and one or more other stitches interlaced over this. Examples are raised chain band, laced herringbone, pekinese stitch and whipped running-stitch.

Couching is a most useful form of stitchery and consists of one or more

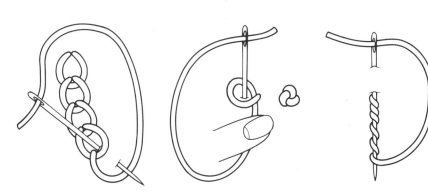

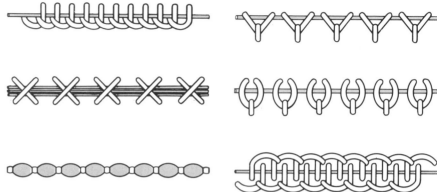

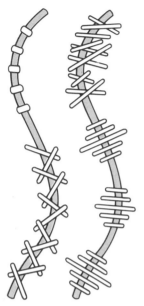

Above
Figures 6.7 & 8
Left to right
Figures 6.9–14

threads laid onto the material and caught down with another thread in a variety of ways, from the basic *straight-stitch* (Fig. 6.7 & 8) through *buttonhole stitch* (Fig. 6.9), *fly-stitch* (Fig. 6.10) *cross-stitch over strands* (Fig. 6.11), *detached chain-stitch* (Fig. 6.12), *thick thread couched together with finer thread* (Fig. 6.13) to intricate *double buttonhole-stitch* (Fig. 6.14).

In *cross-stitch* (Fig. 6.15) the only thing to remember is to keep the top half of the cross slanting one way throughout the work to give uniformity. To avoid starting with a knot, leave a long end when making the first stitch and run this into the back of the stitches once some embroidery has been worked. Finish off in the same way.

Figure 6.15

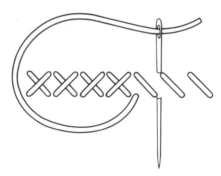

TECHNIQUES OF STITCHERY

Stitchery is divided into various techniques, some of which are briefly described in the following paragraphs. Each technique generally requires different types of threads and fabrics.

Appliqué This is a method of applying one fabric to another by means of stitchery. This can be termed 'onlay' as opposed to 'inlay' where pieces of fabric are set into background fabric. Almost any fabric can be used but, if the article is to be laundered, the materials should be reasonably alike.

The piece of fabric to be appliquéd must match the grain of the background fabric so that it will not pucker. A few tacking stitches will hold it in place while tiny stitches should be used in self-colour thread to hold the fabrics together. If the material frays badly, it is better to allow for a turning. To neaten the edges, a cord or couched thread close to the appliqué, or a variety of edging-stitches, such as button-hole, chain and herringbone, can be used.

Assisi embroidery This form of embroidery is named after a small Italian town, where it was used in domestic and ecclesiastical work. It is a distinctive type of work in which the background is filled with stitchery and the designs, usually of birds and beasts, are left in outline. The designs are worked out on graph paper and counted on even-weave material. As it is a counted thread technique, a tapestry (blunt) needle is required so that the threads of the material are not split. The traditional colours are a cream linen fabric and china blue or crimson cotton threads for the stitchery, with a black thread outline.

Two stitches are used in this work, one being the cross-stitch background. Take care to ensure that the top thread of the crosses lie in the same direction. First, though, the outline of the design is worked; this has the appearance of back-stitch but is, in fact, a running-stitch worked over the same unit of threads used for the background of cross-stitch, say three threads. A return journey is then made along the same line, filling in the gaps left by the first line of stitches. This double running-stitch is called *holbein-stitch* (Fig. 6.16). In order that this stitch should lie flat, the needle is slanted slightly on the return journey as shown in the diagram. If this is not done, you will notice that the stitches will be 'stepped' and an uneven outline will result.

Figure 6.16

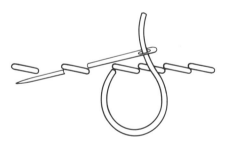

Black-work By implication, this is the name given to embroidery worked in black thread on white material (Fig. 6.17). It found great favour in England during the reign of Henry VIII and, although generally assumed to have been introduced by Catherine of Aragon, and sometimes called Spanish-work, there is a theory that the work may have been adapted from the newly discovered technique of printing and that it was an interpretation of black and white print into embroidery. The designs consisted of scrolling stems with counted repeat filling patterns in the leaves, fruit and flowers. Gilt threads were often used to enhance the delicate stitchery and fine work.

Today, the use of tone is of great importance and this can be achieved either by the use of different weights of threads in one design, or by the subtle change

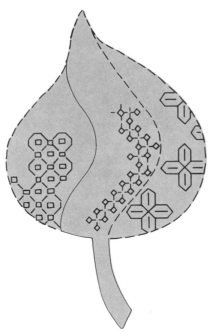

Figure 6.17

of pattern obtained by leaving out a stitch and literally 'fading' the pattern, with more stitches being omitted towards the edge of the shape. It may be helpful to begin a pattern in the centre of the shape and work out to the edges.

The designs are worked by counting the threads on an even-weave fabric and a variety of threads can be used, from the finest sewing cotton to heavier crochet and knitting yarns. A tapestry-needle is used for this work.

Coloured threads can be used, but care should be taken that colour does not detract from the intricate tonal patterns of this technique.

Broderie anglaise or English white-work This is a delicate embroidery technique which at one time consisted only of eyelets varying in size from round holes made with a stiletto to oval shapes cut with fine sharp embroidery scissors. A running-stitch is first made around the outline (Fig. 6.18); the hole is then cut and overcast (Fig. 6.19 & 20). Excess material is turned underneath.

Left to right
Figures 6.18–20

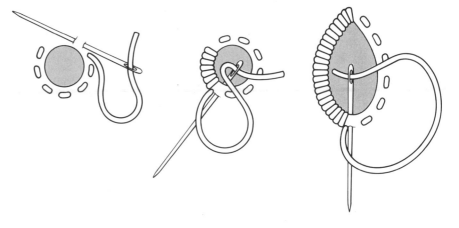

The work was often finished on the edges by scalloping or fine hem-stitching. It was used during the late eighteenth and early nineteenth centuries for ornamenting household linens, underwear and baby-clothes.

Smooth, firm materials, such as cotton, lawn and fine linen should be used, with matching threads in linen and cotton. Fine, twisted embroidery silk can be used with flannel or silk fabrics.

Designs were of a conventional floral nature but, today, a much more textural form of white-work is done, including a number of surface-stitches and contrasting padded satin-stitch with eyelet holes. Stitches used include French and bullion knots, chain-stitch (see earlier) and *stem-stitch* (Fig. 6.21). In *trailing-stitch* (Fig. 6.22), threads are laid on the surface and closely satin-stitched over and through the material. *Padded satin-stitch* (Fig. 6.23) consists of horizontal satin-stitches across the shape, covered completely by vertical satin-stitches. A *raised stem band* (Fig. 6.24) is made from a foundation of long closely packed straight-stitches, tied with evenly spaced right-angled stitches. These are worked over, from the bottom upwards, in stem-stitch so that the foundation threads are completely covered. Finish in the same hole each time to round off the ends. In the *raised chain band* (Fig. 6.25) a button-hole-type stitch is worked over parallel foundation bars. *Rice-stitch* (Fig. 6.26) consists of tiny back-stitches alternating in rows.

Canvas-work This is also known as 'needlepoint' in America and sometimes erroneously referred to as 'tapestry', perhaps due to the fact that some wools used in this work are known as tapestry wools and the blunt needle required is known as a tapestry-needle.

Canvas-work was practised in England during the Middle Ages and reached it's peak of popularity during the late seventeenth and early eighteenth centuries, when it was used extensively for hangings and covering furniture of that period. Berlin woolwork of the mid-nineteenth century, with its crude colours resulting from the use of new chemical dyestuffs, caused the work to fall into disrepute but, thanks to William Morris, it was again restored to its rightful place for hard-wearing seats, stool-seats, cushions, handbags, floor-coverings and panels.

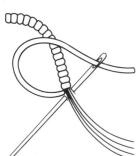

Above
Figures 6.21 & 22
Left to right
Figures 6.23–26

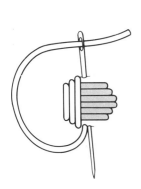 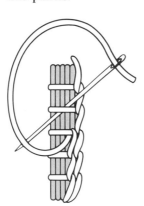  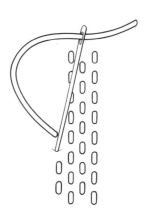

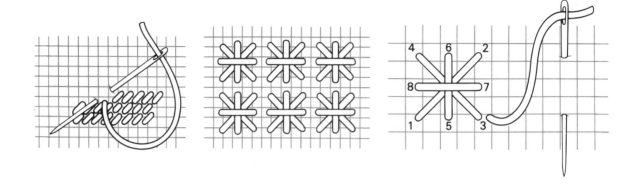

Canvas is made in single or double thread, and is measured by the number of threads to the inch as with even-weave linens. It can be fine, with eighteen threads to 2.5 cm (1 in), or coarse with seven threads to 2.5 cm (1 in) for rug canvas. Single thread canvas is favoured for a free modern approach.

Canvas-work design falls into two distinct types. There is the geometric counted type, using a chart, where the complete canvas is covered with stitches, usually in wools, which is suitable for hard-wearing surfaces on chair seats and ecclesiastical kneelers and rugs. Then there is the free, abstract type of design useful for panels, hangings, boxes, table lamp-bases, handbags and belts.

Exciting textural pieces of work can be developed by drawing directly onto the canvas and using a variety of stitches, including some surface-stitches such as satin, chain, eyelets, French knots, together with the traditional cross-stitch, *tent-stitch* (Fig. 6.27) which can be worked on the diagonal to prevent the canvas stretching, *Smyrna-stitch* (Fig. 6.28 & 29) and canvas-work *rice-stitch* (Fig. 6.30) also known as *crossed-corners rice-stitch*. Fig. 6.31 shows a large cross-stitch worked first in thick thread over four threads of the canvas then in finer thread over the corners of each cross to form smaller crosses. The addition of leathers and beads, and the use of Lurex threads, raffenes, stranded cottons, silks and crochet threads, all add to the richness of this modern approach to canvas-work.

It is advisable to use a slate frame so that the threads of the canvas do not pull out of shape.

Care should be taken with the colour scheme. The texture of the stitches speak for themselves and colour should be considered most carefully.

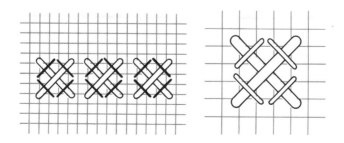

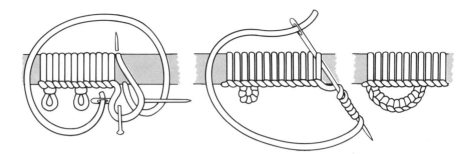

Left to right
Figures 6.32–34

Cut-work This is a form of embroidery where the backgrounds of the design are 'cut' away. Cut-work requires firm linen and is traditionally worked in self-coloured threads, which can be of linen or cotton, with a thicker crochet cotton for padding. Sharp embroidery scissors are essential for the careful cutting away of the fabric.

All designs need careful planning so that the shapes are linked and do not hang loosely after the background is cut away. All the outline of the design should be drawn double and these lines will be a guide for a row of running-stitches just inside each drawn line, which is then closely button-holed with the 'corded' edge of the stitch facing the parts of the design to be cut away. In all cases, the stitchery should be done before any cutting of the fabric.

There are several types of cut-work, from the Simple, where the cut spaces are quite small and need no reinforcing, to Renaissance work, which has larger cut spaces with the addition of button-holed, woven or twisted bars, linking the shapes for additional strength and decoration. Richelieu work is more elaborate with *looped* (Fig. 6.32), *bullion* (Fig. 6.33) or *button-holed* (Fig. 6.34) *picots* added to the bars. Venetian cut-work is further enriched with heavier padded button-holing and padded surface-stitchery. Italian cut-work is remarkably akin to Reticella lace and consists of small squares cut from the fabric, into which geometric patterns are worked by throwing threads from the corners and weaving and button-holing over them, with the addition of surface-stitchery.

Drawn fabric or pulled-work This is a fascinating technique and is worked upon linen where the threads can be easily counted. The background fabric is drawn together by the stitchery and, although the stitches are themselves decorative, a lot of the pattern is dependent upon the spaces, giving the work a rich lacy appearance without weakening the fabric by withdrawing threads. A tapestry-needle is required to prevent splitting the threads. Working threads should be comparable to the thickness of the linen threads and self-coloured. A thicker thread can be used for surface stitches and outlines and heavier crochet cottons are useful.

Designs need large simple shapes for this work, since the drawn fabric stitches are of the 'filling' type. All the filling stitches are pulled very tightly and provide a good contrast to areas of surface-stitchery. This makes the work very textural and it is interesting to see how different one stitch, such as satin-

Left to right
Figures 6.35–39

stitch will appear, when pulled tightly and then worked normally over the same number of threads (Fig. 6.35–39).

Care should be taken to run in the end of the threads carefully on the open filling stitches to avoid crossing the holes and marring the appearance of the work.

There are a great variety of stitches and these are described comprehensively in Mary Thomas's *Dictionary of Stitches* and Moyra McNeill's *Pulled Thread*.

Drawn thread-work This should not be confused with drawn fabric-work through the similarity in name. Drawn thread-work, as it's name suggests, is a form of embroidery which necessitates the withdrawing of warp and weft threads. It is carried out on good quality even-weave linen; the working threads are of similar colour, but a little coarser, for weaving, and finer threads are used for hem-stitching and button-holing. Drawn thread-work is used mainly in the form of borders for domestic articles and is also used for ecclesiastical work.

When preparing the linen for work, a thread is drawn to ensure that the fabric will be straight. Threads are carefully withdrawn to whatever depth of open-work is required, and are finished at the edges, either by overcasting or button-holing the cut ends, or darning the loose threads into the back of the fabric to avoid fraying. If a hem is necessary, the threads can be tacked and eventually

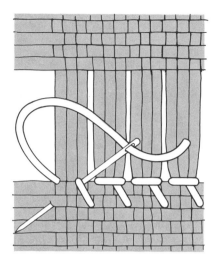 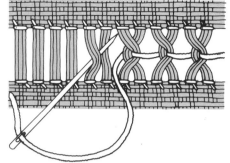

hidden when the hem is turned. The top and bottom edges of the withdrawn fabric are hem-stitched (Fig. 6.40) to strengthen the edges and to conveniently tie the loose threads into bunches to aid the working of the decorative stitches, which consist of twisting or gathering the bars together in various formations (Fig. 6.41).

Needle-weaving, Hardanger and Hedebo embroidery can be placed under the heading of drawn thread work but they are usually categorised separately.

Patchwork and quilting These are covered comprehensively elsewhere in this book—suffice to say that they can be successfully combined with other embroidery techniques. Italian and Trapunto (stuffed) quilting can be most effective in conjunction with the textured embroidery of today.

Shadow-work This is a delicate form of embroidery, popular in the eighteenth century, where the stitching, usually of *closed herringbone*, is worked on the back of fine fabrics such as organdie, muslin and georgette (Fig. 6.42). This gives an appearance of a 'shadowy' effect on the right side of the work (Fig. 6.43).

Other stitches can be used but remember to choose those that can be finished off invisibly, such as feather- or Cretan-stitches. Back-stitch is useful for any linework.

Traditionally, shadow-work is worked in white cotton, stranded cotton or silk threads on white, but brightly coloured threads used on pale transparent fabrics give a most interesting opalescent effect on the right side.

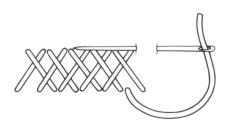 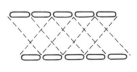

Left to right
Figures 6.44–46

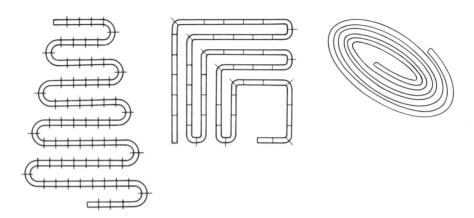

Machine-embroidery This technique has, at last, been accepted as a valid form of embroidery.

An electric or treadle sewing machine is required, for both hands are needed to guide the work. A careful study of the manufacturer's instruction booklet is needed in order to understand the effects that occur when the presser-foot and feed-dog are removed and the tension of the top and bottom threads is altered.

An embroidery ring frame, with the inner ring bound tightly with cotton tape, is required and then it really is a matter of moving the ring frame, holding tightly framed fabric, underneath the needle. Fewer mechanical errors occur when the machine is run at high speed.

To be able to place fabrics onto a background material and add machine line stitches, does help to speed the preparation time spent on developing a new idea and, with the addition of hand-stitchery and perhaps some beads, there is no reason why the completed piece of embroidery cannot be as personal a statement as a piece of work embroidered entirely by hand.

Metal thread embroidery This is a technique using luxurious and exciting threads. Most of the gold threads are laid on the surface of the material and couched down in a variety of ways (Fig. 6.44–46). Jap gold, which consists of a silk core wrapped around with fine strips of gold can be couched, using two strands at a time, with beeswaxed Maltese silk thread (Fig. 6.44). Circular shapes are best worked from the outside towards the centre (Fig. 6.46). Purls, available in a variety of sizes and textures, are made of fine wire, tightly coiled like tiny springs. These can be cut into lengths and used in loops or flat areas as 'bead-like' structures. There are also beads, sequins and gold and silver leathers that can be padded to give a different surface texture.

Gold, silver and copper all come under this category; the pure metal threads are normally used for ecclesiastical work. For experimental work, there are many synthetic threads on the market. Look for metallic crochet yarns, Christmas wrapping threads, cords off chocolate boxes and dress fabrics. For copper, unravel a pot scourer; the inside of a television cable offers an interesting plaited wire which can be opened out, frayed and unravelled. Metal threads can be used with other forms of embroidery to give added interest and highlight on an otherwise matt surface.

Dorset feather stitchery I feel that mention of this work is appropriate, although it is a separate style of work on its own.

In 1954, Mrs. Olivia Pass adapted the designs of the English smocks which were worn for work and leisure for over three hundred years. She taught eighty local ladies her meticulous method of working the stitches and they, in their turn, have influenced and inspired other embroiderers. Her charming little book, *Dorset Feather Stitchery*, gives exact details of the work, involving stitches like blanket, chain and feather and their variations.

NEW WAYS WITH FABRICS

Threads and materials are often hand-dyed or sprayed with dye before being used for embroidery. This offers new and exciting scope. Much of the new work in the art colleges demonstrates the great interest in how the materials react to manipulation, and much time is spent upon experimental samplers, leading to greater understanding of the fabrics.

Materials can be torn, cut, slit, with other materials pulled through the holes. They can be pleated and pin-tucked, gathered, smocked, frayed and unravelled and, if all this seems alien to the traditional needlewoman, take heart, for excellent needlework is still employed alongside this experimentation!

Do not hesitate to use different techniques together. Trapunto quilting and drawn fabric work combine very effectively. Machine-embroidery and surface-stitchery, with the addition of a few beads for additional texture, is interesting.

Above all, do experiment. Embroidery is a rich and exciting craft.

DESIGN

This is a most difficult area to cover, since design can be very personal. There have been many informative books written about design for embroidery in recent years so, to assist the complete novice, I give a few basic tips that may help.

First of all, consider what your design is for. Is it for a panel, box, cushion, place-mat or a detail on a cross?

Let us consider a panel. As a general rule, the eye travels through the design from the bottom left of the centre, so your main point of interest could be placed there. Anywhere off-centre is a good place for a focal point. Padding and heavy materials are best kept at the base of the design. Echo shapes and overlap them to keep a co-ordinated scheme. Link the shapes with line. Lines of stitches or couched threads will give direction. Shapes cut out of one piece of paper will always relate, and this method can be useful as a starting point for design. Look at the spaces between the shapes and the grouping of shapes. They should be just as interesting as the shapes themselves. Simple shapes are best.

A helpful tip when designing and consequently embroidering from a design, is to take a look at the work in a mirror; the reverse image will give an entirely different view and can be of assistance in critically assessing the balance of the design.

Design sources Collect cuttings from newspapers and magazines of anything that catches your eye and appeals to you. A magazine cutting may give suggested texture or an instant design; two L-shaped pieces of card can be cut out to mask out other areas and moved over magazine advertisements, drawings and photographs to find an interesting area from which to trace a design. This can be altered by adding or subtracting lines, re-tracing as required.

Visit museums, art galleries, textile and art exhibitions. Carry a small sketchbook and make rough sketches of ideas for design. Collect natural objects like leaves, bark, shells and stones and make careful drawings of the patterns in them.

Develop an awareness of your surroundings. Look at architecture and natural form and, even if you feel your drawing is shaky, do persevere, because your personal sketchbook does not have to be shown to anyone else and the drawings need only suggest the shapes with a few notes on colour at the side to remind you of the time you saw the original object.

If pencil frightens you, try ballpoint, felt-tip or pen and ink, and you will be surprised to find how much more carefully and confidently you will draw when you know you cannot rub it out!

Colour A knowledge of colour theory is useful. It is preferable to keep your colours closely related in the colour circle so that they do not fight.

Tones of one colour are good, with perhaps a small area of strong contrast. Black, white and one colour is effective. Do not have equal quantities of different colours.

Magazine advertisements are often useful for a guide to colour. Cut out strips for future reference for a colour scheme. Fashion and furnishing fabrics often have interesting and sometimes unusual colour schemes.

After practise with your own design and embroidery, you will have your own ideas and will gradually move away from the so-called 'rules' of design and colour and still be successful.

Transferring designs to material How to transfer your design onto the material depends upon the fabric and method of work you plan to use.

For most fabrics, a method called 'prick and pounce' can be used, where the main lines of a tracing of the design are pricked with a sewing-needle on the reverse side. The tracing is turned over and laid on the material, and pounce, originally cuttlefish bone, but nowadays more often talcum powder (on dark fabrics), or powdered charcoal (on light-coloured fabrics), is lightly rubbed over the pricked tracing. Once the tracing has been carefully removed, the series of small dots of powder can be joined together with a fine paint-brush and thick watercolour paint. When this is completely dry, the excess powder is shaken off, leaving a permanent outline of the design.

Unfortunately, some designs do not always work out satisfactorily from start to finish, so another method, which has the advantage of alteration if necessary, is to trace the design onto tissue paper, pin this onto your fabric and tack through the main lines. Large stitches in a contrasting coloured thread can be used on straight simple lines and smaller running-stitches used where the design is more complicated. Finally, carefully tear the tissue paper away, leaving a rough outline in thread, which can be snipped out after the embroidery is completed.

Transparent fabrics can be laid over the design which can then be traced through with a hard, sharp pencil.

Canvas can also be laid over the design and drawn or painted. Do not use felt-tipped pens for this, as they can smear and spoil the work if the canvas is dampened for stretching after the work is finished. Dressmakers' carbon paper can be used on some fabrics, but follow the instructions carefully.

Projects

CROSS-STITCH SAMPLER

A modern day sampler can be made in cross-stitch. This is not, of course, a sampler of many stitches, but an exercise carried out in one stitch. For the beginner, it may be just the starting point required in order to build up confidence with needle and thread.

Think of the details of your family—particulars of marriages, children, grandchildren, type of house, family pets. If you look at samplers in your local museum, these will give you a guide to setting out your own work. When you have a rough idea, draw the details onto graph paper, blocking out each square to represent a unit of cross-stitches. Always try to centre the important details and balance smaller items at the sides. For example, simple tree-shapes and flowers could give an interesting border to the names and dates of the family. (If a family-tree sampler does not appeal to you, why not consider a map sampler in surface stitchery? This can be of your country or county; perhaps a lasting souvenir of a holiday, or even of the area in which you live, incorporating some of the historical facts and legends that are often forgotten. Some research at the library or local museum into the history could make a very interesting project.)

Do not worry if you feel unable to draw realistically because cross-stitch, of necessity, requires very simple shapes and relies on the shading of the embroidery threads for interest.

Another method of designing for cross-stitch, is to draw the design out on plain drawing paper, take a careful tracing of the design and then transfer this onto a sheet of graph paper. The curved outlines of the original drawing can then be altered to fit the squares of the graph paper and indicate the cross-stitches.

Before you commence the sampler, it is advisable to work a small motif from your graph paper design, taking one square to represent one cross-stitch made up of three threads across and three threads up on the linen to see at what size the motif works out in stitchery. A coarse linen will work up on a much larger scale than a fine one. You can alter the size of stitch by counting over a greater or fewer number of threads, providing that they are the same number across and up on the linen, but do keep to the same sized cross-stitch throughout the embroidery.

Alphabet sampler As a beginning, try the simple design in Fig. 6.47. Using dress-maker's carbon paper, place it between the design and the fabric that

Figure 6.47

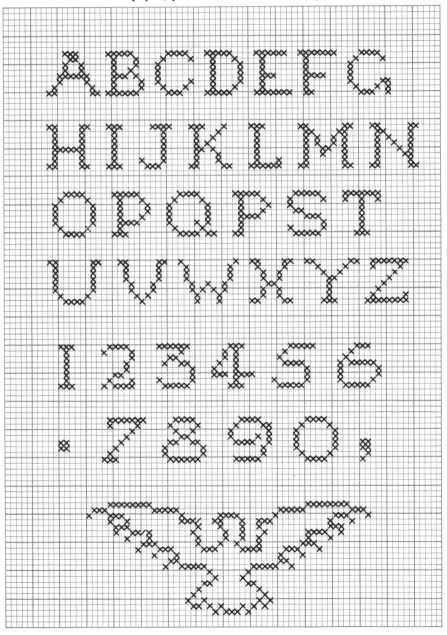

you wish to use. Trace firmly over the lettering so that the outlines will be clearly visible on the fabric. You are now ready to begin the cross-stitch. Once you have mastered this simple exercise you can confidently attempt something more challenging.

STITCH SAMPLER

Small samplers of a few stitches taken from the main groups will help you to understand the character of the stitches as well as their limitations. When you have mastered the basic stitches, try using a different type of thread on a different type of fabric. If you have already tried, for example, a stranded cotton on a firm linen fabric, try a wool on a medium-weight dress fabric and then on hessian. You will begin to appreciate how different the stitches look and how the background fabrics react to the different thicknesses of thread.

Make your stitch samplers interesting. There is no need to stitch straight lines one after the other. Try stitches like button-hole stitch as a wavy, undulating form, opening up the stitch in some places, working closed button-hole in others and varying the size. Stitches can be worked in a circular design or as blocks of stitches, side by side, like buildings on the skyline. French knots can be clustered together and other stitches such as fly-, feather- and cretan-stitch can be worked on top of each other to create texture and depth.

When your samples are complete, make small 'window' mounts in strong card and sticky tape the samples behind these pieces of card. You will be surprised to find how much more interesting the samples appear and they will be a record of your work for reference.

House and garden sampler Using several different stitches and different colours and shades of stranded embroidery cotton, transfer the design (Fig. 6.48) onto the fabric, using either dress-maker's carbon paper or the tissue paper method. Remove the tissue paper, then embroider over the stitches, which may be pulled out when your design is finished. Complete your picture, if you wish, with a border. Place it on a cardboard backing and finish it off by placing a card mount around it, or have it framed, to give the professional touch.

SAMPLERS OF TECHNIQUES

A useful exercise in order to learn the techniques and their limitations, is to design a simple shape and translate this into a variety of methods of embroidery.

For example, a simple leaf shape could be worked in black-work, white-work (Fig. 6.49), surface-stitchery (Fig. 6.50) and canvas-work (Fig. 6.51). Each sample of work will be influenced by the method and materials used. The counted thread samples will be much more stylised than the surface-stitchery.

These samplers need not be large pieces of work and can be window-mounted behind card so that they are a permanent and well presented record of your work.

Figure 6.48

Stitches

1 Stem
2 Blanket
3 Fern
4 Satin with straight
   stitch leaves
5 Long and short stitch
6 Back-stitch
7 French-knots
8 Button-hole

Embroidery is a creative art form and is subject to change with the modern trends. Technique will, however, never change and once the needlewoman has a basic knowledge of stitchery, she will have a limitless source of pleasure. So enjoy your stitchery and experiment with modern threads and fabrics. Above all, have fun!

Left to right
Figures 6.49–51

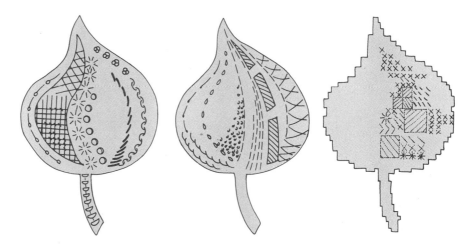

Bibliography

HISTORICAL

Ashton, Leigh, *Samplers*
Jones, Mary Eirwen, *British Samplers*
King, Donald, *Samplers*
Snook, Barbara, *English Embroidery*

STITCHERY

Butler, Anne, *Simple Stitches*
Coleman, Anne, *The Creative Sewing Machine*
Dawson, Barbara, *Metal Thread Embroidery*
Dean, Beryl, *Creative Appliqué*
Geddes and McNeill, *Blackwork Embroidery*
Howard, Constance, *Book of Stitches*
McNeill, Moyra, *Pulled Thread*
Rhodes, Mary, *Needlepoint*
Short, Eirian, *Embroidery and Fabric Collage*
Snook, Barbara, *Embroidery Stitches*
Springall, Diana, *Canvas Embroidery*
Thomas, Mary, *Embroidery Book*
Thomas, Mary, *Dictionary of Embroidery Stitches*

DESIGN

Harding, Valerie, *Textures in Embroidery*
Howard, Constance, *Inspiration for Embroidery*
Liley, Alison, *Embroidery—A Fresh Approach*
Lillow, Ira, *Designs for Machine Embroidery*
Messent, Jan, *Designing for Embroidery from Ancient and Primitive Sources*
Whyatt, Betty and Oxland, Joan, *Design for Embroidery*
Whyte, Kathleen, *Design in Embroidery*

GILLIAN M. GRIFFIN

7 Quilting

THE ORIGIN of quilting is obscured in the depths of the past. Tombs have provided some of our best preserved textiles and one in the USSR yielded a quilted funerary carpet, dating from somewhere between 100 B.C. and A.D. 200. This carpet has many intricate designs of animals and the centre is covered with the scrolling design often associated with Celtic art.

A better known piece, held in the Victoria and Albert Museum, London, is the Sicilian quilt, one of three surviving from 1935. These quilts have a series of pictures of the life of Tristram with a text for each piece of the legend. The aim of this kind of embroidery was to tell a story, to a largely uneducated population, in a form which they could understand. These quilts are made of linen, stitched with brown thread, and padded in the method known as stuffed, or trapunto, quilting. By looking at these old pieces of work you will see that the expertise of the quilter goes back a very long way.

There are records which suggest that quilted jerkins were used as a form of armour from times as early as William the Conqueror. These were effective against the spear and arrow, but, once pistol and cannon shot evolved, the quilted jerkin was reduced to being used beneath metal armour to prevent chafing.

Actual examples of early quilting are extremely rare and most information that we have comes from documents and inventories. We can tell which sixteenth-century materials were used in this way. Sarcenet, or cendal, was a kind of silk sometimes used for the top and lining fabric of quilted items, but mostly they were made of linen. The padding was sheep's wool. For economy, patchwork was used for the top fabric; this was padded with layers of old fabric or perhaps a worn blanket.

Trade with the East in the sixteenth century influenced the use of coloured threads and embroidery on the surface of quilted items. Quilted clothing was worn throughout the century—items such as petticoats, jerkins and headgear—it was considered essential to keep the head warm at night so a quilted nightcap was worn.

There are more pieces of seventeenth-century work existing, especially in the Victoria and Albert Museum, London. Many of our traditional quilting patterns, such as those in Fig. 7.1, can be traced to these items.

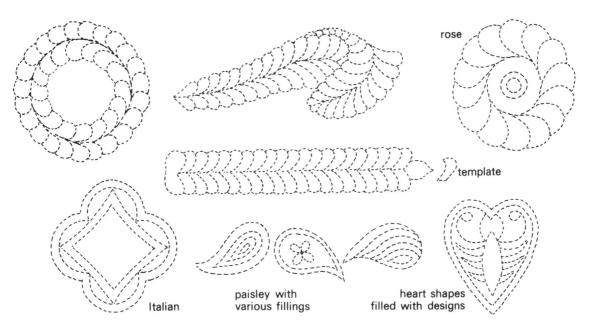

rose

template

Italian

paisley with
various fillings

heart shapes
filled with designs

Figure 7.1

Quilted clothing and bed-furnishings became increasingly popular in the seventeenth century and quilting was also used to line caskets, trunks and coaches. This is possibly the development of upholstery. The Eastern influence in design and colour is still very apparent and the delicate workmanship, up to and including the mid-eighteenth century, is really quite spectacular. Quilting was at its height in popularity, many beautiful items from this period can be seen at the Museum of Costume in Bath. The people who did the work were often professional designers and quilters who lodged in the house while the work was being carried out. Intricate surface embroidery and pulled work were often added to the designs. There are many examples of children's linen caps which show this work in great detail and there was still some thought to economy, as there are several small items, and children's clothing, which were made from 'cut down' larger pieces.

By 1770 the quilted petticoat was no longer fashionable and slowly styles changed and thinner fabrics were used for all clothing. Gay cotton prints were being used for bedspreads and quilting contracted to a few comparatively small areas of the country. In the mining areas of Durham and South Wales, professionals were still making beautiful bedspreads; many of these can be seen in museums of the areas, for example, The Bowes Museum, County Durham, Great Britain.

While the professional quilters of Great Britain rejected patchwork for the upper surface of their work, eighteenth- and nineteenth-century Americans were producing the most beautiful effects using this method. The American Museum in Bath has an extensive collection of these quilts, beautifully displayed and worthy of considerable study.

Patchwork was used primarily for economy, but resulted in the social event of the 'quilting bee', and the production of some facinating quilts. Some of this work is still being carried on today.

The twentieth century brought us the 'eiderdown', so called because its original filling was the down of the eider duck. These were generally made commercially by machine and machine-made goods were gradually ousting the hand-work, some quilted fabric being sold by the yard. Brave schemes during war-times helped to keep the craft alive until two books were written—one in 1930 by Mrs. Hake, called *English Quilting*, and another in 1954, called *Traditional Quilting*, by Mrs. FitzRandolph. These revived the interest in the second half of this century, and we began to wear quilted housecoats and small jackets and some babies had quilted jackets for warmth.

We take for granted now the quilted anorak and sleeping bags of this century, although, more recently, fashion designers have used quilting on collars, yokes and skirt hems.

The quilted bolero has become extremely popular and a few enthusiasts are making hand-made quilts again for a luxury market. Quilting is now done mostly by machine, but hand-work of all kinds has had a tremendous revival, enriching our surroundings, clothing and our lives.

Materials and equipment

top fabric	tracing paper
stuffing	transfers
backing fabric	carbon paper
frames	scissors
threads	thimble
needles	dress-maker's tracing wheel
tapestry- or rug-needle	french chalk
patterns	

CHOICE OF FABRIC

Top fabric A soft, fine-textured silk, cotton or linen, even fine leather, can be used. Very stiff, knitted or stretchy materials are not suitable. Light colours show the quilting to better advantage than dark colours. Luxury fabrics, such as silk and soft leathers and suedes, can be extremely effective.

The centre padding For wadded and stuffed quilting it is possible to use sheep's wool or an old blanket and there is a soft knitted fabric, for the finer materials. New developments in textiles have produced tricel or polyester wadding which can be bought by the yard in fabric shops or department stores. This has the advantage of being washable.

The backing fabric This can be muslin, organdie or mull. It is often useful, for wadded quilting, to make the backing of a lining fabric, or of the same fabric as the front or top, to enable the item to be reversible.

THREAD

This should always be strong and match the composition of the top fabric, i.e., natural thread for natural fibre fabric, man-made thread on synthetic fibre fabric. The colour is normally matching but some modern effects have been produced using different tones or contrasting colours.

NEEDLES

Again, these must be compatible with the fabrics being used, although generally speaking, a long, fine needle will be most suitable for anything with a thick padding. Experienced quilters use the short, 'between' needle, others prefer sharps. It is obviously best to suit your personal preference. It can be useful to thread up several needles at once to avoid interrupting the work too often.

FRAMES

The small, round embroidery frame will be adequate for any small pieces of work and the larger, square table model for cushions or tea-cosies. Anything larger will require a quilting frame. This consists of two wooden bars, called runners, which are the horizontal members. These have webbing attached to them, which must be long enough to accommodate the width of the item being made—228 cm (90 in) for a quilt! They can have slots in them to make the frame a little more adjustable.

The vertical members are called stretchers and, as their name suggests, with the aid of lacing, they help to keep the work taut. Stretchers have holes in them to enable the runners to be adjusted. The work can be done a little at a time and moved upward in the frame as each section is completed.

Basic techniques

DESIGN

It is best to organise the designs of the items to be made, even before buying the fabric. The importance of selecting the right design to suit both purpose and fabric cannot be stressed too much. However good the workmanship, if the designs are bad or incompatible with materials, the finished result will be disappointing.

Small experimental samples of work can help to enable a correct choice to be made; these can be made from pieces in the 'bit' bag and the design kept simple, just to give an impression of the possible final effect.

Everyone has different taste and the choice has to be left to the individual. Only general guidelines can be given, such as the scale of the design being in keeping with the size of the item. Random patterns can create interest with a variation of texture by quilting some areas closely and leaving some unquilted. (The plain areas should not be more than 5 cm [2 in] square or the filling will loosen.) Interesting effects can also be obtained by designing the quilting to fit the shape of the item. This method can also be applied to garments.

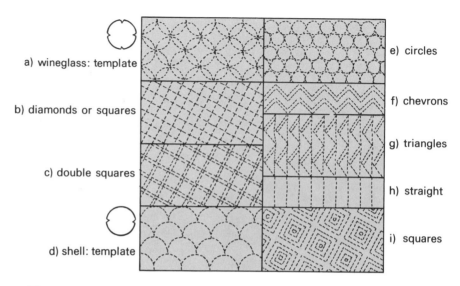

a) wineglass: template

b) diamonds or squares

c) double squares

d) shell: template

e) circles

f) chevrons

g) triangles

h) straight

i) squares

Figure 7.2

The most usual patterns are all-over geometric repeat designs (Fig. 7.2). These can be worked out on squared or isometric graph paper and with the use of templates. Beginners should stick to simple designs and gradually progress to the complicated free shapes, especially if the work is to be done on the machine. Added interest can be obtained with machine-quilting by using satin-stitch and automatic patterns. Always remember that the process of quilting reduces the size of your original fabric and pattern outline. A final piece of advice; begin with a small item, like a belt, bag or tea-cosy, and progress to the bedspread!

MARKING AND TRANSFERRING DESIGNS

(a) Patterns can be drawn directly onto the backing fabric, i.e., mull or organdie. This means that the stitching will be worked from that side; an even running-stitch should look the same from both sides. This is a permanent method of marking.

(b) The outline can be traced through, or template outlined, with a dress-maker's tracing wheel. This would be a semi-permanent method, unless the outline was picked out again with a fine water-colour.

(c) Needle-marking can be used. With a blunt tapestry- or rug-needle, press gently round the outline of template to make an indentation (do *not* scratch) in the fabric. This has to be done little by little as the work progresses as the marks will work out as you sew.

(c) Prick and pounce permanent marking requires tracing paper, French chalk and a large needle. Trace the design to be used onto the paper with a fine pencil, then *turn the paper over*, or the design will be reversed. Prick out the outline of the design with the needle—the paper will have to be on a soft surface to do this—an ironing board is ideal. Now turn the paper over, showing the rough side of the holes. Place it in position on the top fabric and fix or hold it firmly. Next, gently press through French chalk powder or a similar fine powder, with a small soft pad. A strip of felt rolled into a tight coil is suitable for this.

When the tracing-paper is lifted, the design can be clearly seen but must be painted over with a fine water-colour line for permanence. This process is more complicated than others, but it is always accurate and especially useful for the more complex designs.

(d) Long straight lines can be marked with a chalked string which is held tightly at both ends, the middle of the string can be 'pinged', by picking it up and letting it drop sharply, thus producing a line. Outlines can be drawn with chalk directly onto the fabric but do make sure, by testing on a spare piece of fabric, that the chalk will rub off. This is a semi-permanent method.

(e) Carbon paper, transfers or direct drawing onto the top fabric will be a permanent method of marking, suitable for some fabrics and some methods of work. Great care must be taken to ensure that the stitching covers the outline; a running-stitch, for instance, will not.

TACKING

All upper and lower fabrics must be ironed before commencing work.

All quilting has two or three layers of fabric which must be secured together as one while the work is in progress. This is done by tacking closely to ensure that they stay together and do not move. Any movement after the work has begun will make unsightly ridges and pulls. You cannot be too generous with your tacking.

The whole of the item must be tacked before the quilting is begun, unless the fabric is so fine that it would mark badly. Silk, for instance, or velvet, must, in this case, be secured with very fine needles used as pins.

On small pieces of work, tack from the centre outward, beginning with the vertical and horizontal lines, then continuing into the corners (Fig. 7.3). On larger pieces, a grid pattern would be more suitable (Fig. 7.4).

Left to right
Figures 7.3 & 4

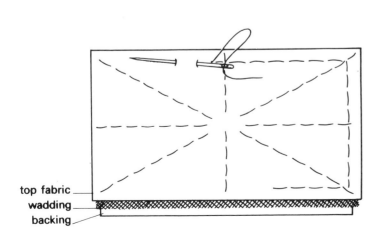
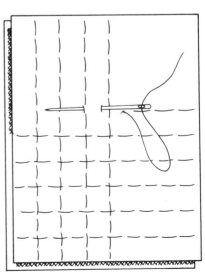

top fabric
wadding
backing

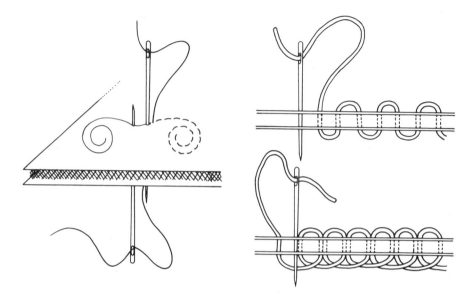

Left to right
Figures 7.5–7

If you are using a frame, fasten the backing to the frame first, then tack the upper layers to it. Then treat the layers as one piece of fabric.

STITCHING

Stitching should be done with an up and down movement (Fig. 7.5); this is essential for a good result. Stitches used traditionally are: running-stitch, back-stitch, pearl-stitch and, sometimes, chain-stitch or the quilting knot (Fig. 7.6–10).

FINISHING

Selection of the methods of finishing will vary according to personal taste and the item being made.

Left to right
Figures 7.8–10

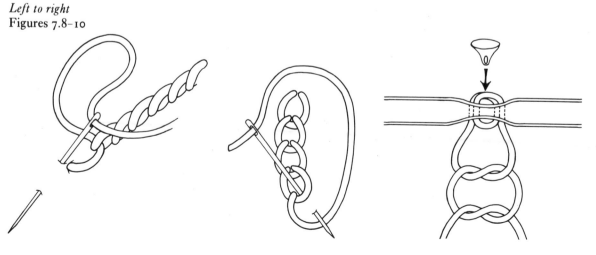

Edges These can be bound, piped or finished with a decorative satin-stitch on the sewing-machine, and the excess fabric trimmed away after sewing. It is effective, if there is an acceptable backing fabric, to trim away the wadding and upper or top fabric to a level where the backing can be brought over to the front of the work and machined down; mitre the corners. Alternatively, both backing and top fabric can be folded in towards each other and a neat line of machining placed along the edge.

Seams Wherever possible it is best to trim away any padding from seams to reduce bulk. For reversible garments, a flat fell or strap seam is best. This latter seam is achieved by sewing a ribbon or binding over the raw edges of a plain seam, when they have been opened out and pressed flat.

One of the best seams for a quilted garment is to make a plain seam with the top fabric alone, right sides together. Trim away any wadding, then fold in the backing fabric sewing this down invisibly by hand.

Choose pattern styles without gathers or fullness and cut all sections of the pattern singly.

TYPES OF QUILTING

There are several methods of quilting which, in the course of time, have been given various names. They have been named after the method used, the effect obtained or the supposed country of origin. To describe the method of work I shall use the name which seems to be the most apt.

Wadded quilting Sometimes known as English quilting (although the Welsh and Americans are also renowned for their work). This is a method of sewing together three different layers of material—top fabric, filling or wadding and backing—to provide a warm textile for clothing and a comfortable upholstery in the home.

First iron fabrics for top and backing. Plan the layout and the design carefully, using paper patterns and tracings. It is important to remember that the process of quilting reduces the size of the original fabric because of the undulations resulting from the sewing. Extra allowance must be made for this, and the paper pattern must be checked against the work after the quilting has been carried out. This phenomenon is known as shrinkage. Tack all the layers together carefully, keeping the fabric flat and, wherever possible, smoothing out from the centre of the work. If a frame is to be used, sew the backing fabric onto the webbing first, then smooth the padding and top fabric over it. Now tack as before. Finally, lace the sides of the fabrics to the frame.

Now is the time to needlemark or chalk any semi-permanent method, just as much as can be carried out at any one time.

Work the stitches following the up and down movement to keep the layers of fabrics absolutely flat and keeping carefully to the outline marked. The quilting knot can be used instead of running-stitches and should be placed at intervals to secure the wadding.

When all the quilting has been completed, remove the tacking; any additional embroidery can be done now. The item can now be constructed in the normal way.

Stuffed quilting Sometimes known as trapunto quilting (Fig. 7.11), this method uses only two layers of fabric, a top fabric and a loosely woven backing—mull or linen scrim. The padding is pushed through this backing with a crochet hook or small openings are cut in the backing and sewn up afterwards. Stuffed quilting is often used in conjunction with other types of quilting to give emphasis to a particular part of the design. In this case the stuffed quilting should be done first. It can, however, be very effective on its own as the Sicilian quilt proves. The padded shapes need to be kept in organised groups, otherwise a bitty effect will result.

Iron the fabrics and transfer the design, if a permanent method is to be used. Fix the backing into the frame or spread it out on a flat surface and place the top fabric onto it. Tack the layers thoroughly (*a*).

Semi-permanent methods of marking can now be used, marking each section just before it is to be sewn. Quilt-stitch round the outlines of the design to be padded (*b*).

Remove the tacking-stitches and, from the wrong side of the work, ease the backing threads apart and push in small pieces of padding, a little at a time, using a crochet hook or a small blunt implement (*c*). Make sure that there is enough padding to lift the area sufficiently from the front and that it is evenly padded. Now ease the backing-threads back into place.

For larger areas of padding, a small slit may have to be cut in the backing to insert the padding; this can be oversewn together afterwards. As all stuffed quilting must be lined, the appearance of the backing is unimportant.

Corded or Italian quilting This is a similar principle to stuffed quilting in that only two layers of fabric are involved (the top and the backing) and the padding is inserted after the stitches are worked (Fig. 7.12).

Left to right
Figures 7.11 & 12

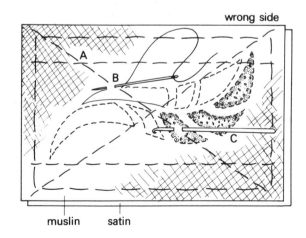

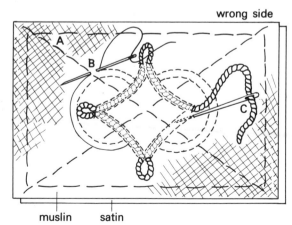

The designs for corded quilting must all consist of two parallel lines of running- or back-stitch. Between these two lines is threaded a cotton cord, rug-wool, Italian quilting wool or suitable knitting wool. Care must be taken to ensure that these filling cords are pre-shrunk and colour-fast.

Iron the fabrics and mark the design onto the top, or backing if a permanent method has been selected.

Place the top fabric over the backing, right side up, and tack closely (*a*). If using a frame, sew the backing to the webbing first and then proceed with the tacking. Now work the quilt-stitching, either running- or back-stitch, along the parallel lines (*b*), until the design is completed. Remove the tacking and turn the work over to the wrong side. Thread a tapestry- or rug-needle with the cord or wool selected, using just enough to complete one section of the design and to fill the space between the parallel lines. Now push the needle into the backing only and between the two lines of stitching, pulling the wool through the space as you might thread an elastic through a casing. Where there are sharp corners or angles in the design, bring the needle out through the backing and take it back again at the same point, continuing along the design but leaving a small loop of cord at the angle negotiated (*c*). Continue with this until all the parallel lines are filled. Turn the work to the front to see the final raised effect. The work can now be lined and made up in the usual way.

Corded quilting can be worked on a single piece of fabric by making a herringbone-stitch over the top of a firm cord from the wrong side of the work (Fig. 7.13). Great care must be taken to keep the stitches even on the right side, where a neat back-stitch should be seen.

Figure 7.13

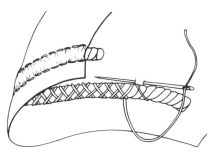

Shadow quilting This can be produced by either of the two previous methods described, merely by altering the materials used. A transparent top fabric, for example, organdie, voile or fine silk, can be threaded or stuffed with brightly coloured wool (colour-fast). This will produce a delicate pastel shade through the surface of the top fabric—extremely effective where colour is required as well as texture.

Machine quilting All types of quilting can be worked on a sewing-machine. Large items are rather unwieldy and it may be better to quilt them in sections. The pieces can be joined together afterwards, either invisibly, where the quilting design can be fitted into the seam, or decoratively, using an embroidery stitch.

The type of needle and thread used will depend entirely on the fabric, a good idea is to make a sample from the materials being used and try out different sizes of thread and stitch until the desired effect is obtained.

With wadded quilting make sure that the layers are securely tacked. Loosen the pressure on the presser-foot if the top fabric is being pulled. The motion of sewing by machine often pushes the upper fabric through slightly faster than the lower one. To avoid this effect distorting the shape of the fabric, work alternate rows of quilting in opposite directions and hold the fabric firmly either side of the foot. Figure 7.14 also shows the gauge being used to keep the stitching straight.

On the machine, if the presser-foot is removed and the feed-dog lowered, free stitches can be worked in any direction. This needs a great deal of practice and the fabric must be held firmly in a frame.

Flat quilting This is a method of giving strength and decoration to a fabric without the bulk of a filling. It is worked in the same way as wadded quilting, omitting the centre padding. Chain-stitch is sometimes used in this work to outline the design.

Pillow quilting This is where quilting overlaps into patchwork, the distinction I have made between them is that there is a padded or quilted effect given by this form of patchwork and quilting, produced in one operation. The easiest way to describe this is to suggest you visualise a series of small bags lightly stuffed with wadding (Fig. 7.15), or chopped-up tights. The bags are then sewn together either with an embroidery stitch or neat oversewing (Fig. 7.16).

Suffolk puffs These are also closely allied to patchwork but again a padded effect is obtained, this time without the use of wadding. Circles of fabric are cut in a fine, soft cotton or silk. The circles should be just a little more than twice the size of the finished patch.

On the wrong side make a hem all round the edge of the circle and run a

Left to right
Figures 7.14–16

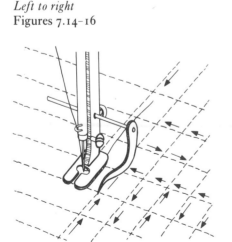

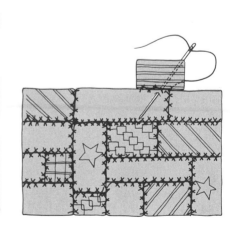

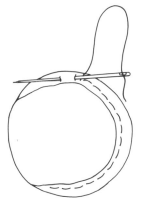
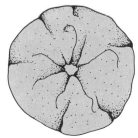
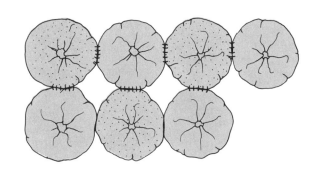

Left to right
Figures 7.17–19

gathering-thread through it (Fig. 7.17). Pull up the gathers tightly into the middle of the patch and fasten off very securely (Fig. 7.18). Press gently, making sure the gathers radiate evenly from the centre of the patch. Sew the patches together from the wrong (ungathered) side with a few neat oversewing stitches (Fig. 7.19).

The whole work will need to be mounted onto a backing to give it sufficient strength to withstand use.

Left to right
Figures 7.20 & 21
Below
Figure 7.22

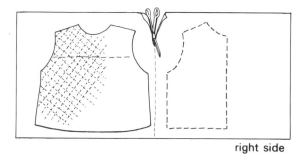

right side

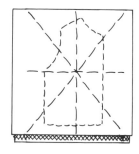

Projects
WADDED QUILTING BOLERO AND POCKETS

Lay the pattern on single outer fabric and tack around the pattern to give an outline. Cut the material into rectangular sections for easier working of large pieces (Fig. 7.20). Small pieces, such as the pockets, can be quilted then cut out.

Tack the wadding and lining to each section (Fig. 7.21) as described previously. Quilt by hand, sewing-machine or both.

The outline will have been reduced in size by the quilting so, using the pattern again, cut out the bolero.

Sew the side and shoulder seams, trimming away the wadding. Bind the edges and the seams to neaten and make ties. Bind the pocket edge and sew in place (Fig. 7.22).

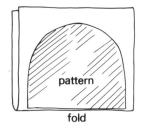

WADDED QUILTING TEA-COSY

To avoid a seam around the bottom edge of the tea-cosy, proceed in this way. Draw a paper pattern—the average size is 36 × 30cm (14 × 12in), but, for greater accuracy, measure the pot, remembering to allow for the padding.

With the pattern to the fold of the fabric cut two pieces (Fig. 7.23).

Open out the fabric and tack, firstly thick wadding, and then muslin or mull, on half of each piece (Fig. 7.24).

Work a design on each half section (Fig. 7.25). With right sides together, tack then machine the two pieces together, leaving an opening at the bottom edge (Fig. 7.26). Remove tacking.

Pull up the lower unpadded section of fabric over the padding and neaten the top edge (Fig. 7.27). Turn the completed cosy to the right side (Fig. 7.28).

As you can see, there are many forms of quilting, whether you choose traditional designs or modern variations. Its use can provide decoration, warmth and comfort.

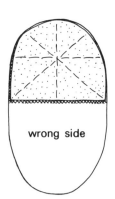

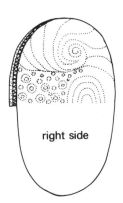

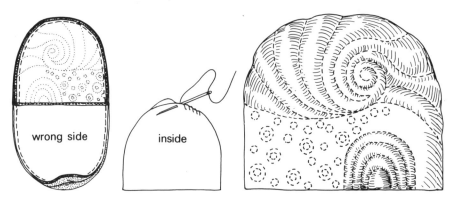

Above
Figures 7.23–28

Bibliography

Colby, Avril, *Quilting*
Short, Eirian, *Introducing Quilting*
Snook, Barbara, *Embroidery Stitches*
Thomas, Mary, *Embroidery Book*
Whyatt, Betty and Oxland, Joan, *Design for Embroidery*
And also:
Embroidery Magazine
The Needleworker's Dictionary
Weldon's Encyclopaedia of Needlework

GILLIAN M. GRIFFIN

8 Patchwork

THE WORD 'patchwork' is inevitably linked with quilts but either can be worked independently to great advantage. I have endeavoured to show this in the chapter on Quilting. We will now take a closer look at patchwork, beginning with the patchwork quilts which gave the work its popularity.

Patchwork has been worked in Britain for two hundred and fifty years, although, sadly, it seldom seems to be considered of any value, as quilts have been discovered rotting in sheds and under mattresses. For this reason, very few pieces remain. There are, luckily, some treasured heirlooms of the days when the household would own, for each bed, a winter quilt, a summer one, one for best and one for visitors. Many of these would be patchwork for economy reasons.

In America, most famous of all for its patchwork quilts, a young girl would be expected to own thirteen quilts by the time of her marriage. These were begun as soon as she could sew, and her marriage quilt would be the last and best. References to these quilts date as far back as 1692. Patchwork was used because the thrifty life of the early settlers demanded no waste. The quilts could often tell the story of the family clothing, as patches were made from every scrap of outgrown, and the better parts of worn, clothing.

The American-style patchwork is made from square blocks, geometrically divided. The geometric designs of the blocks are pieced together and the blocks joined together afterwards. Some of these designs handed down by the Pilgrim Fathers, are often identical to those in Great Britain, just the names vary. One design can have names like 'Windy Walk', 'Indian Trail', 'North Wind', 'Flying Dutchman', in different areas of Great Britain, Canada and the USA. A large number of these quilts can be seen in the American Museum in Bath. They are hung like pages in a book, to enable the viewer to examine them closely.

Patchwork has been described as a salvage art; it was certainly born out of thrift and the need to repair, to patch, and to conserve small pieces of valuable fabric which had no use unless stitched together to make a new whole. Therefore, it is assumed to have begun as a peasant craft.

Perhaps it was the extremely precious nature of gazelle hide that prompted the making of the earliest surviving piece of patchwork in B.C. 980, now housed in a museum in Cairo. It was certainly more economical to decorate garments with pieces of fabric—appliqué—instead of using the expensive damasks or embroidery threads of the sixteenth century. Examples of appliqué are more common than mosaic patchwork, although one piece of the latter was found in the Cave of One Thousand Buddhas in India, showing a technique, used in 600–900 A.D., which is still being used today, namely oversewing small geometric shapes together.

Appliqué can be seen in many of the houses open to the public. Hardwick Hall in Derbyshire has some sixteenth-century wall-hangings made by the Countess of Shrewsbury, 'Bess of Hardwick'. It has been suggested that some of the fabrics used for this were from vestments no longer needed by the church.

It is certain that patchwork was made by, and sold for, the prisoners in Newgate prison, London, although not a trace of this seems to have survived, even in Australia, where relatives of those unfortunate people were found.

There are huge gaps in our knowledge of the history of patchwork, due to the fact that so little has survived. Two of the earliest materials used in Britain were chintz (from the Hindi word meaning 'variegated') and calico (from Calicut on the south-west coast of India) which were imported when trade with the East opened up in the seventeenth century. These fabrics became so popular that an embargo was put on their importation; this, of course, made them more valuable and the small pieces left over from furnishings were used as patchwork. A fine example of this is in Levens Hall in Kendal—a complete four-poster bed-hanging and quilt, made in 1708.

Great Britain eventually began producing its own chintz and calico and, by 1800, the price was brought down considerably, bringing it within reach of more people. The need for patchwork therefore declined.

One of the social graces of the nineteenth century was embroidery, and patchwork was included in this; even Jane Austen is reputed to have made a quilt, but, by the turn of the century, it was out of fashion again. Crochet and macramé were the thing! There was less need for economy, except in the traditionally thrifty areas in the north, although there are one or two examples of the fashionable crazy patchwork, rather inferior in design and construction.

With the advent of World War 1, patchwork nearly died out altogether because of women going out to work. But there were always a few people keeping it going, whether out of need or enthusiasm. There are one or two enthusiasts still living who can remember making quilts in the 1920s. Their quilts survive to prove their expertise. One of that era was a Mr. Walter White, who stitched together over 17,000 patches to make a most striking coverlet (while on night-duty for Midhurst District Council).

To raise money for charity in the 1930s, groups of people began making quilts again and so there was a revival, continuing during World War 2, making hospital bed-covers. Scarcity, expense and clothing coupons were to make textiles a valuable commodity again and patchwork was used to make dressing-gowns, waistcoats and even slippers; economy rather than appearance was the main concern.

More recently, in this century, patchwork has been recognised for the beautiful creative art that it is and church vestments, quilts and clothing of fascinating design have been produced. In Great Britain, Women's Institutes, the Embroiderers' Guild and evening classes put on by the local authorities have been largely responsible for this revival but it would not have materialised without the desire of people generally to create beautiful handiwork.

It is interesting to see pieces of patchwork, both old and new. It may be necessary to make an appointment or ask to see special pieces. The Victoria and Albert Museum and the Embroiderers' Guild in London, have a fine collection, also the Royal Scottish Museum in Edinburgh. Many local establishments also keep a few pieces, such as the dressing-gown in the Kings Lynn Museum and the door curtain in Bamburgh Castle, Northumberland, made by Russian prisoners, from their uniforms, during the Crimea War.

One patchwork quilt, in the Red House Museum in Christchurch near Bournemouth, has embroidered on it a motto which could be adopted for all patchworkers: 'Keep a thing, its use will come'. Of all handicrafts, patchwork has to be one of the cheapest to take up. It is of great satisfaction to make 'something from nothing', and the gentle rhythm of oversewing the small patches together can be positively therapeutic.

Materials and equipment

suitable fabrics	sewing needles
templates	thimble
graph paper	scissors for paper and fabric
thin card or stiff paper	pencil—H or HB
threads	

Patchwork is one of the simplest of all handicrafts, needing virtually no equipment and using odd scraps of material cut into various patterns by means of templates shaped as squares, rectangles, hexagons and lozenges, etc. Shapes are then joined together, either by machining or oversewing, to make, for example, a complete garment, bag, bedspread or tea-cosy. Scraps may also be appliquéd onto a plain material and made up into an article of clothing, a cushion-cover, or even curtains. The variety of things you can make is immense (Fig. 8.1); a little imagination as to materials, colours and shades, together with the shapes to be incorporated, can produce a very attractive finished article.

In planning your work it is important to visualise the end product. A patchwork of haphazard colours and fabrics can have a particular charm, but patchwork which has been planned carefully, in terms of fabric, colour and shapes, will have the professional appearance of a work of art.

CHOICE OF FABRIC

Firstly, you must select your fabrics; these should be of equal weight and thickness. Also consider the texture—sometimes an interesting weave can add

Figure 8.1

variation to plain colours and prints. The fabrics should be sound and of good quality, especially if using second-hand materials. The easiest to use are crisp cottons or not too springy polyester–cottons. Do not use material that frays or is easily marked, although it is possible to make patchwork from silk, spun rayon, or even velvet, once you have become accomplished. All materials should be pre-shrunk and sound. It is extremely important that you have enough material at the outset to complete your design.

Figure 8.2

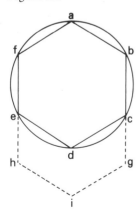

TEMPLATES

Metal templates can be bought from most needlework shops and department stores. They are expensive, but normally come with a transparent 'window', useful for cutting out fabrics with a printed design which needs to be placed in the centre of the patch. It is possible to make your own templates. These must be geometrically accurate, otherwise your patchwork shapes just will not fit together.

Hexagon (Fig. 8.2) With a pair of compasses set at a radius equal to the required length of the sides, draw a circle on thick card. With the compasses at the same setting, place the point anywhere on the circumference and make a small arc to intersect the circle at *a*.

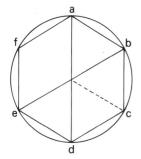

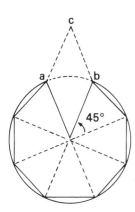

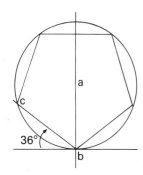

Above
Figures 8.3–5

Place the compass point at *a* and make a further arc on the circumference at *b*. Continue around the circumference in this way until six arcs have been made. The last should cross at *a*. Join the intersections with straight lines and cut out the shape with a sharp knife and a steel ruler.

Elongated hexagon (coffin) (Fig. 8.2) Proceed as above, but extend sides *bc* and *fe* the required distance to *g* and *h*. With compasses set as above, draw arcs from *g* and *h* to intersect at *i*. Draw lines *gi* and *hi*. Cut out.

Lozenge/diamond (Fig. 8.3) When pierced together this shape will make a 6-pointed star. It can also be used for three-dimensional boxes. Draw a hexagon as above and draw lines *ad* and *be*. Cut out.

Triangle (Fig. 8.3) This shape can be made from half a diamond or half a square.

Long diamond (Fig. 8.4) An 8-pointed star can be formed from long diamonds. With the compasses set at half the length of the diamond, draw a circle. Draw lines, at intervals of $45°$, from the centre to the circumference. Join the intersections to form an octagon.

With the compasses at the same setting, place the point at *a* and make an arc outside the circle. With the point at *b*, make another arc to intersect the first arc at *c*. Draw lines *ac* and *bc* to complete the shape. Cut out.

Pentagon (Fig. 8.5) Draw a base line and a second line at right-angles to it. With the compass point at *a* and radius *ab*, draw a circle to 'sit' on the base line. At an angle of $36°$ to the base line, draw a line from *b* to intersect the circle at *c*. With the compasses set at a distance equal to *bc*, mark off the circumference with arcs as before. Join the intersections to give a pentagon and cut out.

THREADS

Two sorts of thread are required, one for tacking and one for oversewing. The oversewing should be done in one overall colour wherever possible. Use synthetic thread for synthetic fabric and natural thread for natural fibre. The hard synthetic threads cut through a natural fibre.

Basic techniques

One can divide the most common methods of working patchwork into three groups:

a) mosaic patchwork, which is worked in distinct geometric shapes over paper templates.
b) American-style 'block' method, where square 20–30cm (8–12in) blocks are made up from geometric shapes with the use of paper patterns. The squares are then joined together afterwards.
c) machine patchwork of various types.

DESIGN

Bear in mind always the colouring of your patchwork; this can make or mar your finished article. Try to visualise and make a rough drawing of the overall colour effect you wish to achieve, for example, a pale blue centre to purple edges, or individual squares of red and white, alternating with black and white. A three-dimensional effect can be obtained using diamonds (Fig. 8.6) and the varying colour density of printed fabric is shown in the hexagon 'flower' (Fig. 8.7). Patterns should be arranged to give balance within each unit and within the overall design. Try out different schemes and choose the best for your needs. Remember that tone, variation of colour from dark to light, is particularly effective and, of course, consider the environment in which the finished work will be placed.

This rough drawing can be broken down into smaller workable units and shapes. The use of square or isometric graph paper is invaluable for this process. Your choice of shapes will be guided by three things:

(a) the amount of time or work you are prepared to put into it. Large shapes for example will be quicker and entail less work than small ones. Machine patchwork will be quicker still.

(b) the thickness of the fabric. Thicker fabric generally requires larger shapes. Sometimes it is possible to make the shapes fit a particular printed design like the hexagons in Fig. 8.8. These have then been interspersed with plain diamonds.

(c) the number of shapes you wish to use, for instance, hexagons and diamonds, or squares and triangles. Graph paper is essential for working out these and also the American-style block patterns.

Left to right
Figures 8.6–8

There are two choices of working method if you are making a patchwork garment. Either make up a large piece of patchwork, enough to take all the

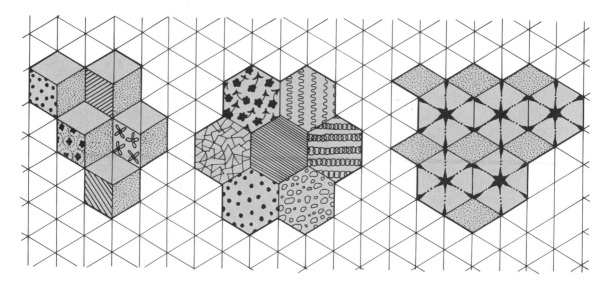

pattern pieces, then make up in the usual way; or make individual sections large enough to take just one pattern piece, for example, the back of a jacket. In this way the patchwork colours can be so arranged that a particular colour is at the centre back and the two shoulders identical—more complicated, but effective.

Mosaic patchwork This is probably the most common method and certainly one of the oldest.

First, plan and select your fabrics. Press all the fabrics to be used. Make several paper templates by cutting around the metal or card template on to stiff paper accurately. This is important if the fabric patches are to fit together properly. The fabric patches are cut next. They must be 1 cm ($\frac{1}{2}$ in) larger than the paper all round to accommodate turnings. The patchwork will be more stable and lie flatter if the grain of the weave goes in the same direction over the whole piece of work. If you are using a patterned fabric, a window template is very useful. This is either of transparent plastic, with the seam allowance shown as an opaque area, or of card cut to the size of the patch, including the seam allowance, with the centre part of the template removed to enable you to see the fabric. Thus it is possible to arrange the fabric so that a particular part appears in the centre of the patch, a flower for instance. This, repeated over the whole piece of work, will give it a continuity of design. The arrangement of a print can sometimes conflict with keeping the grain of the weave the same. When this happens, choose the design; the weave is of secondary consideration. Draw round the outline of the template and cut out the patches.

Below
Figures 8.9 & 10

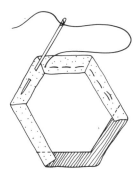

Next, the fabric patches are tacked to the paper templates. Place the paper in the centre of the wrong side of the fabric patch and pin. Thread a needle with tacking thread, fold over the seam allowance and tack through all thicknesses, beginning with a back-stitch, not a knot, and taking especial care to keep the corners neat (Fig. 8.9). Large stitches are best; remember the tacking and paper will have to be removed after the oversewing is done. If your fabric is one which marks badly, do not pin and tack only through the seam allowance and paper, by keeping the needle flat against the work. Tack up several of these patches until you have enough to begin oversewing them together as part of your planned design.

Take two adjacent patches and place them right sides together. Take a needleful of thread in a colour compatible with most of the work—no knot again. Begin by oversewing the end of the thread closely. The corners of the patchwork or the beginning and end of the seam are the weakest points; a knot would easily pull through, so oversewing is more secure at both these points (Fig. 8.10). Oversew, keeping the needle at right-angles to the seam, thus making the smallest stitch on the right side of the work (Fig. 8.11). It is perfectly acceptable to continue to the next patch or seam with the same thread (Fig. 8.12), provided you make those few extra stitches at the beginning and end of the seam.

Carry on tacking up patches and oversewing them together until the work

Left to right
Figures 8.11 & 12

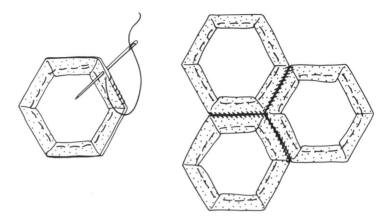

Below
Figure 8.13

9-patch block
front

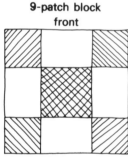

back

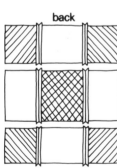

back

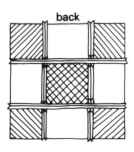

is complete. The paper templates can be removed by undoing the tacking once the patch has been oversewn on all sides. If this is carefully done, the papers can be used again, provided they are in good shape; an iron can sometimes renovate them sufficiently, but throw them away if they are torn or badly crumpled.

When the work is complete, press the seams gently with the tip of the iron on the wrong side as they were tacked. The right side can be pressed lightly but beware of the imprint of the seam allowances showing through. Test a corner first and use a soft ironing-board pad. The work is now ready to be made up.

American-style 'block' patchwork This was born out of the early settlers' existing knowledge of English patchwork and their need for economy.

It is done without the use of paper templates. The shapes are obtained with the use of a paper pattern which can be used over and over again.

The item to be worked in this way is first divided into squares of regular size. The American quilts, for instance, are based on a square of 30–45 cm (12–18 in).

Having decided upon the size of the square you intend to work on, make a paper pattern this size and then decide how it is to be divided up for patchwork. There are literally hundreds of different patterns. You could use the same one throughout, or perhaps two alternating squares. For more designs, consult the *101 Patchwork Patterns* by Ruby Short McKim.

Make your pattern by cutting up the square of paper into the shapes chosen. It is quite a good idea to make a tracing first so that you are sure of the way it goes together again. For accuracy, draw round the paper shapes with tailor's chalk on the wrong side of the fabric to mark the sewing line, and cut out, leaving a seam allowance. As with mosaic patchwork, it is best to keep the grain of the weave one way. If you have planned your design carefully, it will be possible to cut out all the pieces required for the whole piece of work at one time.

The square blocks are now 'pieced' or sewn together individually. Press the seams open as you go. In the old days, of course, this was all done by hand but,

**windmill
front**

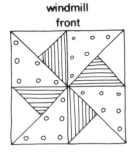

back

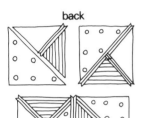

back

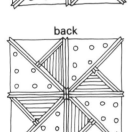

Above
Figure 8.14
Below
Figure 8.15

with careful planning of the order of work, it is possible to do this by machine (Fig. 8.13 & 14).

When making a coverlet or bedspread, make up enough of the square blocks for the whole quilt, then join these into strips the full width or length of the quilt. Next, join the strips together to make the completed quilt. The same would apply to a cushion-cover in which either smaller square blocks or only one block would be used.

Amish quilts The Amish settled in America in the eighteenth century, a religious group driven from Switzerland and Germany for their beliefs. Even today they do not use modern products, such as cars, telephones or television. Some do not even have buttons on their clothing. They made patchwork quilts in the block method just described, but their fondness for plain design and clear, bold colour made them distinctive. A quilt may have a maximum of four colours, many only two or three, and the designs are clear-cut and simple (Fig. 8.15).

Seminole patchwork This is derived from the work of the Seminole Indians in Florida, USA. Their costumes, which they make themselves, have bands of interestingly-made patchwork which have great potential if developed to the full.

The work is done by sewing strips of fabric together first. This can be done on a machine. These strips can be of any length and width, depending upon the finished result required. For the beginner, try tearing cotton into strips about 5 cm (2 in) wide—cotton will usually tear straight when it is difficult to cut evenly. Sew them together with a plain seam. Having done this, press all the seams one way (Fig. 8.16). Now, cut across your strips horizontally, about the same width as before. Keep them all right side up and move the strips about; for instance one up and one down to give a patchwork effect (Fig. 8.17). Now the strips can be joined together again when you have chosen the design you prefer. Sew the new seam in the same direction as you pressed the previous seams; the turnings will lie flat if you do this. Press the whole work and

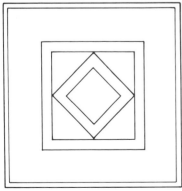

centre diamond

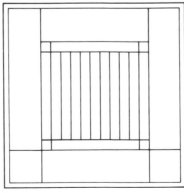

bars

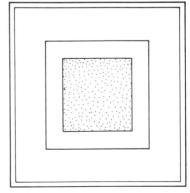

centre square

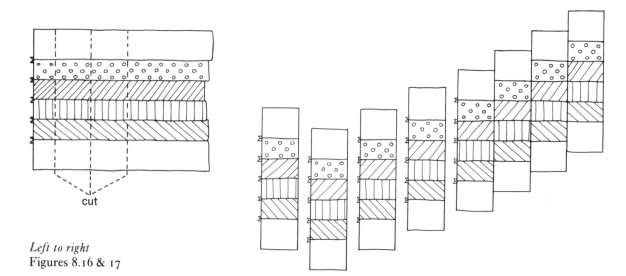

Left to right
Figures 8.16 & 17

it is ready to be made up. Depending upon how you arrange the strips, the Seminole Indian bands can have the minimum of wastage.

Log cabin patchwork As the name suggests, this type of patchwork, which can also be done on a machine, is constructed in a way which resembles the building of a log cabin. The work has therefore been associated more with America and Canada. It has been worked in Great Britain, however, where it is known also as ribbon or log wood patchwork.

Begin again with strips of fabric. This time they must be of equal width. The width of your ruler would be suitable to begin with. You will need a selection of fabric designs, paying particular attention to dark and light tones of colour, which this type of patchwork traditionally utilises to great effect.

The work is carried out on a backing material as a rule. This can be omitted for the experienced worker but it does give the work a greater stability and strength. The backing can be cut from calico or any sound, used fabric in pieces about 15 cm (6 in) square for a cushion, and up to 45 cm (18 in) square for a bedcover.

Select a fabric which is going to be the centre square of your patchwork. This can be a bright colour, plain or an interesting design, obviously matching the strips you intend to use and a similar size to the width of these. Tack this square to the centre of the backing fabric (Fig. 8.18). Now make a crease in one of the strips lengthwise, just the depth of the seam allowance, e.g., 1 cm ($\frac{1}{2}$ in). Place this strip, right sides together and edge to edge with your chosen centre square. Sew along the line of the crease for the length of the square. Cut off the rest of the strip (Fig. 8.19). Press this first strip back to hide the seam and show the right side of the fabric.

The next strip is sewn in the same way, making the crease first as a sewing guide and placing it at right-angles to the first strip, along the bottom edge of the square and across the base of the first strip (Fig. 8.20). Fold back and press.

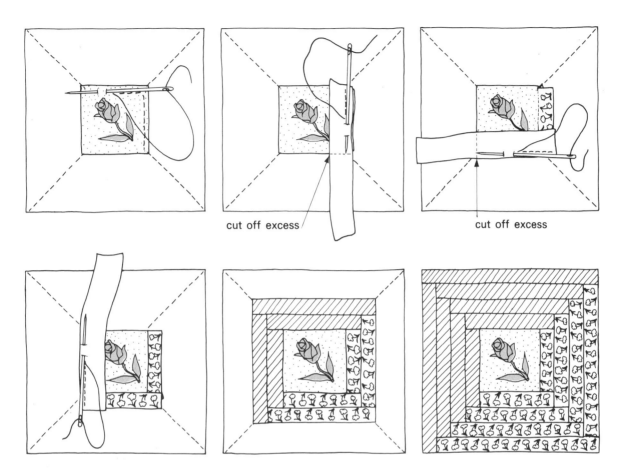

cut off excess

cut off excess

Left to right
Figures 8.18-23

Build up the strips in this way until the block of patchwork of the required size is made (Fig. 8.21 & 22). The colours are traditionally placed with dark strips on one side of the square and light on the other (Fig. 8.23). The arrangement of these squares of dark and light areas can vary the overall design; for example, all the light corners placed together, or all the dark ones, or alternate. In this kind of patchwork, ribbon has the great advantage of being an even width, omitting the need to cut strips.

Crazy patchwork There was tremendous enthusiasm for this type of patchwork towards the end of the Victorian era. Some of it is rather inferior, being composed of too many types of fabric and heavily embroidered. The end result looks far too overworked.

Apart, perhaps, from choosing a colour scheme, no preparation of the patches is necessary, the obscure shapes being part of the design. It is only necessary to trim off any frayed or very rough edges.

A lightweight backing fabric, the shape and size of the finished article is necessary; this can be new fabric, or pieced together, used cloth. The patches are placed on the backing with each succeeding patch overlapping the raw edge of its neighbour. They are tacked in place, keeping the whole work

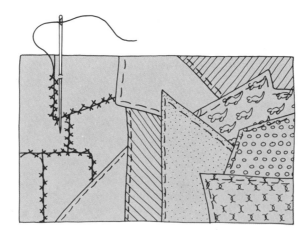

Figure 8.24

absolutely flat. Then the raw edges which are showing are decoratively stitched down. Feather-stitch is one of the traditional methods, but, with a sewing-machine, either a close zigzag or one of the embroidery stitches could be used. The whole item is built up in this way until the backing fabric is completely covered (Fig. 8.24). It can then be assembled in the usual way.

Appliqué work This is included as a patchwork technique, as it makes use of scraps of fabric, applied or sewn on to a background fabric as the name suggests.

A good quality backing fabric is necessary because it will show, and have to withstand, the sewing of pieces on to it. Colour is also important, it must neither dominate the finished product nor be so uninteresting that it does not complement the pieces applied to it. An interesting weave is always a good choice, especially for a wall-hanging; obviously the function of the item to be made is the guiding factor.

Having selected your backing fabric, experiment with small pieces of toning and contrasting colours and textures of fabric in the area to be decorated, until you find enough to give a pleasing effect. Perhaps some threads of various textures will help to build up an idea.

Ideas for designs can be taken from illustrations in books, taking perhaps a part of a picture, not necessarily copying in detail. Natural objects are another obvious source of inspiration, leaves, flowers, birds, etc., again bearing in mind the function of the finished piece and its environment (Fig. 8.25-27).

Try cutting up coloured paper shapes and placing them on your backing fabric to make an interesting design. The paper shapes can be used as pattern pieces for your appliqué.

Fabrics which do not fray—felt, knitted textiles, etc., will not be so difficult

Below
Figures 8.25-27

to sew to the backing as ones which do fray. These will either have to be turned in around the edge, a process not possible with a complicated shape, or they can be closely stitched with a hand embroidery stitch, satin-, button-hole-, feather- or herringbone-stitch. Alternatively, they can be sewn round on a sewing-machine, using a close zigzag or an embroidery stitch.

Appliqué is often embellished afterwards with embroidery stitches, beads, even stones and shells have been used. This is not essential but can add interest to some pieces of work.

Note: It can be an advantage to hold the fabric shapes in place with a fusible fleece prior to sewing them to the backing.

FINISHING AND MAKING-UP

The neatest way to finish off the edges of a piece of patchwork is with a piping cord, covered with a cross-way strip of a matching fabric. The cord should be preshrunk and the cross-way strip cut wide enough to go over the cord, leaving a 1.5 cm ($\frac{3}{5}$ in) seam allowance both sides of the cord. This strip is folded in half, right side out, the piping cord placed in the fold and the fabric tacked over it close to the cord (Fig. 8.28). The *existing* seam allowance along the edge of the patchwork must now be opened out. Use the crease mark left in the work as a stitching guideline.

Now place the prepared piping cord along the edge of the work with the cord on the inside of the creased seam guide, tack along just below the crease (Fig. 8.29). Sew on, either by hand or by using a zip or piping foot on the sewing-machine, making the stitches as close to the cord as possible. The lining can be sewn on by hand afterwards, or stitched by machine with right sides together, sewing close to the cord again and leaving an opening to turn the work through to the right side.

Left to right
Figures 8.28 & 29

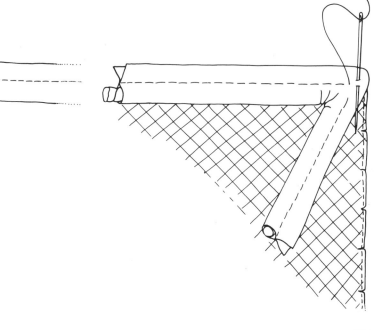

Figures 8.30 & 31

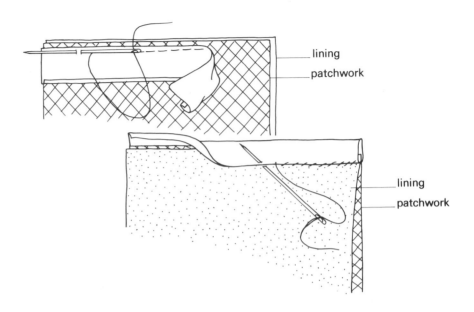

Figures 8.32 & 33

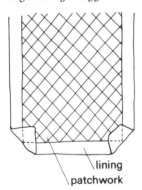

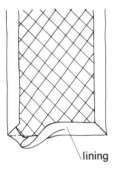

All patchwork must be lined because of the series of seams on the back. The lining can be tacked on to the back of the work and a binding or corresponding material or braid sewn over the edges to neaten them (Fig. 8.30 & 31). Alternatively, the lining can be made larger than the patchwork and the edges brought over to the front, turned under and sewn down (Fig. 8.32 & 33) or the reverse of this, the patchwork taken round to the lining and stitched down. Fringes or frills can be added or inserted into the seam where this would be pleasing.

If a garment is being made and the pattern pieces cut from a large sheet of patchwork, care must be taken, especially with hand-made patchwork, when cutting through the stitching; these seams will have to be fastened off or the work will come unsewn. Having done this, the pieces can be made up in the usual way, using a plain seam. Press the seam allowance open and line the whole garment.

Projects
SEMINOLE INDIAN PATCHWORK SKIRT

Prepare a band of patchwork, as described on pp. 103–4, of the desired width and sufficiently long to go round the skirt bottom. Angle it at 45° (Fig. 8.34) and insert it into the skirt at the desired level. Add ric-rac braid to finish it off (Fig. 8.35).

LOG CABIN PATCHWORK CUSHION COVER

Make four squares of patchwork (Fig. 8.36) about 15 × 15 cm (6 × 6 in), as described on pp. 104–5, and join them together in an attractive design (Fig. 8.37). Cover a piping cord with a matching cross-way strip and sew it to the

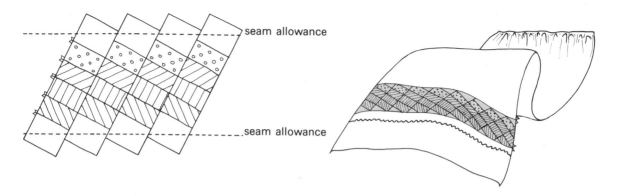

seam allowance

seam allowance

Left to right
Figures 8.34 & 35

right side of the cushion, clipping the corners and neatly joining the ends (Fig. 8.38). Sew a backing to the patchwork, right sides together, leaving an opening for the turning (Fig. 8.39). Turn, neaten the open edges and sew a zip into the opening (Fig. 8.40).

A BOX FROM FABRIC AND CARD WITH A PATCHWORK OR APPLIQUE LID

Careful planning is needed if the box is to be successful.

A box should be firm and have a well fitting lid. The lining and the fastening must be considered as a part of the whole design. Seams must be neat and accurate. Fabrics must be chosen carefully, not loosely woven, or they will distort or the card will show through. The purpose of the finished box will dictate size, materials and shape.

Fittings for the box should be considered, e.g., for a work-box, pin cushions, needlecase, etc., can be made. For best results the pieces should be assembled in the correct order.

Left to right
Figures 8.36 & 37

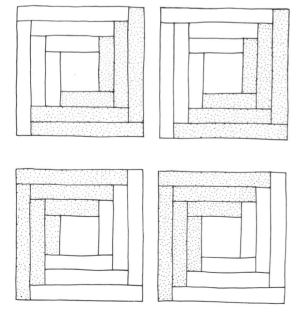

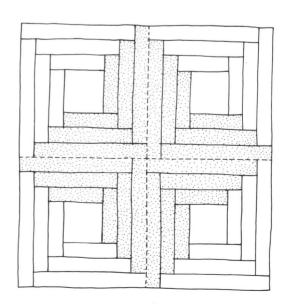

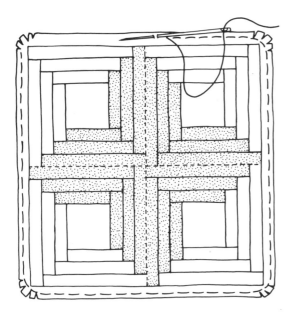

Figures 8.38-40

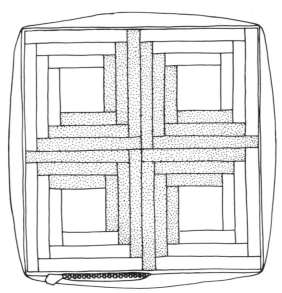

Materials Thick card, up to 2.5 mm ($\frac{1}{10}$ in) thick, thin card, polyester wadding, outer fabric covering including that for the decorated lid, lining fabric to blend with outer cover or provide surprise element, matching threads, invisible thread, pins, needles (possibly a curved needle), thimble.

Method The box is made from the base upwards. Fabric grain lines should be planned in keeping with the shape of the box.

Cut the card for the base, squaring the corners accurately. Now cut the fabric for the base, and lace it on, pulling the fabric taut and keeping the

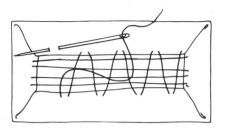
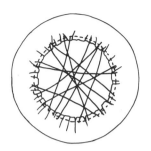
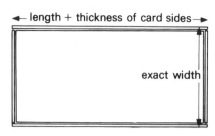

length + thickness of card sides

exact width

Left to right
Figures 8.41–43

corners neat (Fig. 8.41). A gathering thread helps with a circular box (Fig. 8.42).

Measure the sides of the box (Fig. 8.43). The thickness of the fabric can alter the measurement; this is why the base is covered first. A rectangular box can have the short sides set into the long sides, thus the measurement must include the width of the card.

Glue the wadding to one side of these pieces of card. Cut a length of fabric the same length as all four sides together, plus turnings, and the width plus turning and lace this fabric over the side sections, putting the wadded side towards the fabric and slotting in each section as you come to it. The sections can be worked separately but this will give four seams up the sides of your box instead of one. Sew the corner join with invisible thread, pinning carefully first through the card, as shown in Fig. 8.44 & 45. Sew the sides to the base, pinning as before, placing the sides over the edges of the base (Fig. 8.46).

Measure the base of the interior of the box for the lining. Cut this in thinner card. Pad and lace the fabric over it as before and place it inside the box. Measure the interior again for the side linings, these can be in thin card for an overlapping lid or in thick card if the lid is to be a flush fit.

If the lid is to overlap (Fig. 8.47), make the lining 50 mm ($\frac{1}{4}$ in) shorter than the inside of the box. If the lid is to have a flush fit (Fig. 8.48), the lining must stand up at least 1.5 cm ($\frac{5}{8}$ in) (Fig. 8.49) above the outer sides to accommodate the lid. These pieces are covered and padded in the same way as before, making sure the lining fabric comes well down the outer edge of the rim made for a flush-type of lid. Glue or sew into place.

At this stage, a tray support can be stitched into the lining by making another lining shape to fit inside the one just completed. This piece would be about half the depth of the sides—or allowing enough room at the top to accommodate the size of the tray required.

Left to right
Figures 8.44–46

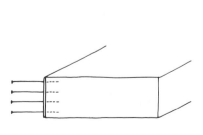
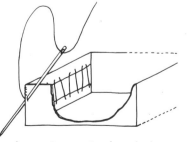
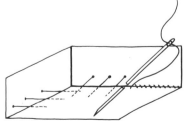

box cut away to show lacing

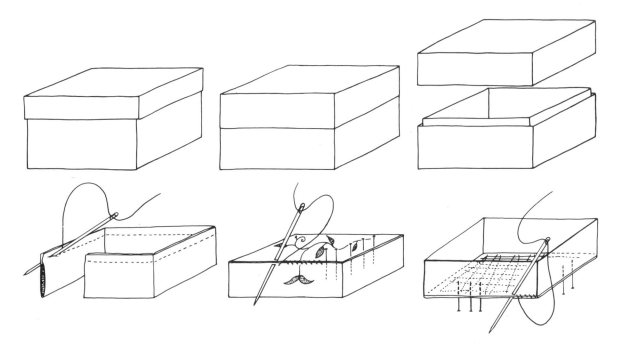

Left to right
Figures 8.47–52

Measure around the box for the lid lip. If the lid is a flush-type, the measurement will be the same as the base sides. Cut card to measurement. Stick wadding on to the outside of the card. Cut a strip of fabric twice the width of the lip or sides, plus a 4 cm (1½ in) seam allowance and the length of all four sides, plus 4 cm (1½ in) seam. Cover the lid lip by doubling the fabric lengthwise over the card sections and back-stitch through the turnings (Fig. 8.50), pulling the fabric very tightly and slightly towards the inside of the box lid. Join the corner.

Measure the outside edge of the lip for the lid, taking the measurement to the outer edge of the card, covering the side edges completely—roughly 1 cm (⅜ in) larger than the base. Make a decorative lid in patchwork or appliqué (Fig. 8.51), beaded or embroidered. Pad and lace it to the card as before (Fig. 8.52).

Place the lid on the lip, pin and sew it with invisible thread, keeping the seam allowance of the lip on the inside of the lid. Make a lining for the top of the lid, padding and lacing as before. Stick it in place, catching the corners only with thread.

Figure 8.53

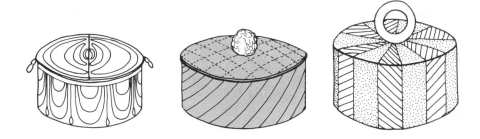

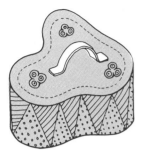

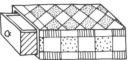

Figure 8.54

The interior tray is made in the same way as the rest of the box, by measuring, cutting, padding and covering, as before.

A round box will require thinner, more flexible card which can be shaped or small ones can be cut from a wide fabric roll. The lining for this will fit better if the fabric is cut on the cross. Lids can also fit inside the box or lie on top (Fig. 8.53).

Boxes can be made almost any shape (Fig. 8.54) with care and planning.

One of the great advantages of patchwork is that it involves little or no initial outlay. It can be worked by young and old alike as the techniques are relatively easy. It has been elevated in recent times to a work of great beauty in the making of church vestments, but the humble quilt is still one of the most popular and rewarding things to make.

Bibliography

Clabburn, Pamela, *The Needleworker's Dictionary*
Colby, Avril, *Patchwork*
Laury, Jean Ray and Aiken, Joyce, *Creating Body Coverings*
McKim, Ruby Short, *101 Patchwork Patterns*
Nield, Dorothea, *Adventures in Patchwork*
Richardson, Rosamund and Griffiths, Erica, *Discovering Patchwork*
Thomas, Mary, *Embroidery Book*
Timmins, Alice, *Introducing Patchwork*
And also
Golden Hands Book of Patchwork and Appliqué

PAMELA MURRAY

9 Candles

THERE ARE drawings on tombs which indicate that the ancient Egyptians were the first to use a primitive candle. This may have been the case; however, we can be certain that the Romans used candles because examples of candelabra, with spikes to take candles, have been found in Pompeii and Herculanium.

The Roman festival of Februa, when candles were carried through the streets and women observed purification rites, was superseded in the fifth century by Candelmas Day, which was observed on 2 February as the Feast of Purification of the Virgin Mary. This was the time when women who had borne children the previous year went to church, bearing lighted candles, to give thanks.

Much mystery and superstition surrounded the burning of candles. Important events could be foretold—a death in the family was imminent if the candle flame guttered or a spot of soot was seen on the wick. Tallow curling away from the flame was known as a 'winding sheet'.

Until the middle of the eighteenth century, beeswax and tallow were the only two materials used in the making of candles, but in the villages of England at that time—and no doubt elsewhere—wives of farm labourers made their own rush-lights. This they did by gathering rushes during the summer, stripping off all the green peel, bar one narrow strip, and leaving them on the ground to bleach in the sun. They were then dipped, one at a time, in boiling fat or grease obtained from the butcher. Costing very little, and burning for 30 minutes or so, they provided the only light in the home—imagine children today trying to do their lessons by such inadequate lighting!

Candles were used for various purposes apart from in the home. Units of time, for example, were measured by the use of striped candles, which burnt from stripe to stripe every 30 minutes. King Alfred, so the history books tell us, after many experiments found that a candle containing 12 pennyweight of wax, burned for exactly 4 hours, so he had candles made that would give light for 24 hours. These were kept burning in churches and the passing of each hour was marked by the ringing of bells. An effective primitive clock! Miners in the old days wore a candle fixed in their hats as their only source of light. Bidding at wine sales and auctions used to end when a pin dropped from the candle. Ritual candles—beautiful and ornate for Christmas and other festivals —are known to us all.

Once philosophers thought that the candle reflected an image of humanity: the wax corresponding to the body, the wick to the mind, and the flame to the spirit.

Today, with the ever-increasing cost of fuel, the romantic candle still holds its own, because of the enchantment of its gentle flickering light.

Materials and equipment

mould seal or plasticine
wicks, sizes 13mm ($\frac{1}{2}$in) to
   102mm (4in) plus
wicking needles
paraffin wax
beeswax sheets and discs
stearin
wax whitener
various coloured dyes
14gm ($\frac{1}{2}$oz) bottles of perfume
thermometer
2 to 3 large saucepans

2 enamel jugs
cheese grater
skewers and cocktail sticks
medium-sized metal pudding basin
scissors
breadknife or hacksaw
metal tea-strainer
kitchen-timer
roll of sticky tape
close-woven cloths
newspaper

WICKS

These are made from plaited cotton or bleached or woven linen thread and then soaked in a chemical solution which, when burning, facilitates oxidation of the wick. It is essential to choose a size of wick that corresponds with the diameter of the candle as it is this that determines whether or not the candle will burn successfully. Wicks are graded in half-inches, according to the diameter of the candle, and range from 13mm ($\frac{1}{2}$in) to more than 102mm (4in). If the mould in use is not of a comparable measurement, it is possible to drop down a size, e.g. 38mm ($1\frac{1}{2}$in) wick for a 51mm (2in) diameter candle. Generally, however, keep to the wick size suitable for the mould which you are using. Commercially produced moulds are made to specific diameters; it is with make-do moulds from containers found in the home that there may be a choice between two sizes.

The correct wick size is important because, when the flame meets the surrounding wax, the absorbent wick, through capillary action, draws the wax upwards, where it is burned off, and, in this way, the flame is constantly fed the correct amount of fuel. If the wick is too small it will tend to burn down in the centre of the candle, eventually drowning in its own pool of wax. On the other hand, if the wick is too large, the walls of the candle will soften and collapse, allowing the molten wax to trickle in an unsightly mess down the side of the candle, over the holder and on to the furniture. This, of course, can also happen if the candle is placed in a draught, when the flame, blown continually to one side, may cause a breach in the candle wall.

A wicking needle, similar to a large darning needle, will be required. Needles come in varying lengths from 152mm (6in) to 279mm (11in) and with eye sizes to take all sizes of wicks from 13mm ($\frac{1}{2}$in) to over 102mm (4in).

WAXES

Beeswax This is the oldest and purest wax and, although costly when bought in sheet form, it nevertheless makes the most beautiful of all candles*i* Coming in a natural shade, honeycombed in pattern, it has a rather pleasant smell of of honey. Beeswax may be obtained as blocks or slablets, which are either yellow or bleached white, or as discs that can be added to paraffin wax to improve its appearance and to give a superior, longer burning candle.

Paraffin wax This refined wax is obtainable in powder form, droplets or blocks, and also in various grades, but, for the making of candles at home, it is best to buy a wax that has a melting point of between 57°C (135°F) and 60°C (140°F). You will find initially that powdered wax is easier and simpler to use. Save all small pieces of old candle stubs and melt them down again with some new wax or bits of your failures. However, it is advisable not to use multicoloured pieces of wax, except for floating candles, as you will end up with a most unpleasant muddy candle! Another thing to remember, which is of help when melting bits and pieces of old candles, is to let the resultant wax cool and then to remove the residue of wicks and any other foreign matter, so that you end up with reasonably clean wax; of course, this can then be used to make further candles.

If any doubt exists as to the absolute cleanliness of the wax, then it is worthwhile filtering the molten wax through a strainer into the prepared mould. Taking into account that the bottom of the mould will be the top of the candle, there is nothing more aggravating than removing a lovely candle from the mould, only to find that sinking dirt and dust particles are embedded in the wax around the wick, thus spoiling the look of the finished article.

ADDITIVES

Several things may be added, though not necessarily together, to paraffin wax before you start making a candle. Of these, stearin is essential.

Stearin A flaky type of wax, this is used for several reasons: dissolving dyes, facilitating release from the mould, as it acts as a hardener, and giving opacity to white and coloured candles. When used in the proportion 1 to 10 with paraffin wax, a very satisfactory and slightly longer burning candle results, which will maintain its shape well and polish to a good surface sheen.

Wax whitener By using a 5% concentration, this makes an excellent substitute for stearin when using rubber moulds and aids opacity, particularly when making pastel shades. When making water candles it is advisable to include 1% plastic additive to your casting as this is a good strengthener; also the candles will burn longer.

Wax dyes These come in powder form and discs, in several colours. A word of warning here as to strength: too much dye and you will fail to have a glowing candle, so it is better to experiment first by putting a small amount of dye into the wax and, when it has melted, to place a drop or so into cold water; when set you will then see whether or not it is the desired shade. If not, simply add more dye. Bear in mind that a small pinch of the powdered dye will colour about 0.6 l (1 pt) of wax, and one disc will produce a strong colour in about 2 kg (4½ lb) of wax. By using more or less of either powder or disc you can get the exact shade you require. Mixing colours is helpful as you will find you are able to get a wider range. The discs are more accurate in their colour, although the powdered colours are cheaper. If you can afford the former, so much the better. There is also a range of pigments which are suitable only for dipping as they are lightfast, but rather difficult to dissolve.

Perfume Lastly, we must not forget that perfume adds tremendously to a candle's attraction; there is nothing simpler than to add a drop or so to the wax, at the correct temperature, just before you pour it into the mould. There are many different perfumes obtainable in liquid form and a 14 gm (½ oz) bottle is enough for about 9 kg (20 lb) of wax.

Figures 9.1 & 2

Another way in which perfume is prepared for the hobbyist, is as discs, which combine colourant with fragrance. These discs are made basically to complement a set of rubber moulds which can be used to make a bowlful of fruit candles. These are apple, pear, orange, lemon, pepper, tomato, pineapple and grapes, the latter, either singly or in a bunch both black and green; they look very realistic, the assorted perfumes are delicate on the air. A rather ingenious room freshener! When the perfumes seem to have vanished, if you burn these unusual candles, still an elusive aroma will be released from the melting core.

MOULDS

Most craft suppliers have a fairly wide range of moulds made from rubber, plastic, glass or metal. They come in a variety of shapes and sizes and are either rigid or flexible.

The most popular candle size is the block cylinder style (Fig. 9.1) of 51 mm (2 in) diameter and it is useful to know that a 114 × 51 mm (4½ × 2 in) mould takes 284 gm (10 oz) wax, while a 165 × 51 mm (6½ × 2 in) mould takes 0.45 kg (1 lb) wax. Candles with a shaped top (Fig. 9.2) are known as point cylinders.

If you wish to obtain a smooth finish to your candle then glass or metal moulds are the most suitable but do take care when handling and filling glass moulds.

The flexible moulds are embossed with different designs, giving a highly decorative candle. These are very suitable for the beginner as they are both inexpensive and strong. It should be remembered, however, that rubber moulds are damaged by stearin so be careful not to use more than 1% of stearin in the wax. Rubber moulds also tend to be sucked out of shape as the wax shrinks but this can be avoided by constantly breaking the skin which forms over the setting wax with a cocktail stick or skewer. Always dry and dust rubber moulds thoroughly before putting them away. When using plastic moulds, care must be taken regarding the temperature of the wax as the moulds will melt or become deformed above 93°C (200°F).

Basic techniques

The making of a good candle is quite an art, as well as an absorbing and inexpensive hobby; once you have the basic equipment, many lovely designs and shades of candle may be made.

Five methods are employed in the making of candles: dipping, moulding, pouring, drawing and extrusion, but here we shall concern ourselves only with the first three methods.

PREPARATION OF THE WAX

It is advisable to melt the wax/stearin mix by the double container method; this prevents the wax from going above 90°C (200°F). At higher temperatures, offensive fumes are given off and, at approximately 204°C (460°F)—flash-point—the vapour given off will burst into flames. Should this happen, put a lid or a large plate over the pan, remove it from the heat and leave for 10 minutes.

Have a large saucepan into which a metal pudding-basin or tin can [0.8kg (28oz) size] will stand; put about 0.45kg (1lb) wax/stearin mixture into the can or pudding-basin and pour water *carefully* into the saucepan to about half-way up the sides of the wax container. Bring the water gently to the boil and keep on the boil until all the wax is melted; it will take about 45 minutes for this amount of wax to reach a pouring temperature of 85°C (185°F) plus. Be

Left to right
Figures 9.3–5

sure not to let the saucepan boil dry; a kettle of boiling water to hand is essential for topping up. When adding boiling water to the pan, use a funnel, thus ensuring that no water splashes into the can of molten wax.

If at some later stage it is felt necessary to bring the wax to temperatures higher than 85°C (185°F), then a thermometer is absolutely essential. The wax need never go above 148°C (300°F); in fact a higher temperature will completely decolourise a pot of dyed wax.

Warnings Take your time and do not rush things. *Never* let wax overheat because of the danger of it vapourising and exploding. If the door bell or telephone rings, turn everything off—electricity or gas taps. *Do not* leave pans on unattended stoves that have not been turned off. *Never* allow children to experiment with candle-making unless under strict supervision. Watch temperatures all the time. When making the candle do not allow a single drop of water on the wick as this will ruin it and prevent it burning.

PREPARATION OF THE MOULD

While the wax is still melting, prepare your mould. If you are using a plastic container, such as a washing-up liquid bottle, cut it, with a breadknife, hacksaw or scissors, to the height of the candle you wish to make (Fig. 9.3). Make two cuts or slits—a 'V' shape will do nicely—in the top of the container, diametrically opposite each other, to support the skewer or cocktail stick.

Heat the point of your wicking needle and pierce a hole in the centre of the base of the container. Remember, nearly all candles are made upside-down, so that the bottom, which will be nice and flat, will actually be the top of the candle.

Ascertain the diameter of your mould and choose the wick accordingly. Thread the wicking needle and feed it through the hole in the bottom of the mould or container, leaving 76mm (3in) or so of the wick standing out. Attach the other end of the wick by tying it to a skewer or cocktail stick; place it across the 'V' slots, pull the bottom 76mm (3in) of the wick taut, bend it to one side of the hole and fasten it with sticky tape. Cut off any surplus wick, say over 25.5mm (1in), then bend it over on to the sticky tape; stick another piece of tape over this so that the wick stays taut. Seal the hole with mould seal or plasticene (Fig. 9.4). Make certain that the wick is central by pushing it along with the skewer.

Dip the base of the mould into some molten wax to waterproof the wick and then stand the mould in a shallow dish of water. Place a layer of pebbles in the bottom of the dish to steady the mould (Fig. 9.5).

MAKING A CANDLE

By now the wax in the basin should be almost ready. Add the colour required, either powder or gratings from the disc. One tablespoon of gratings per 226gm (8oz) of wax will give a pleasant shade of the chosen colour; add more colourless wax or more colour gratings, depending on whether pastel or deep colour is desired. If using candle perfume, 1 drop per 28gm (1oz) of wax, just before pouring the wax into the mould, is enough to give the wax a pleasant aroma without being overpowering.

Fill the mould to the brim with the molten wax—it should be noted here that wax shrinks during the cooling process so after about 30 minutes, it will be necessary to reheat the wax in the pan and top up the mould. Also remember to tap the mould occasionally to make certain that any bubbles in the liquid wax have risen to the surface before the wax begins to set.

Again, after 30 or 45 minutes, topping up will be necessary. Here the timer will be an invaluable reminder. You should now also prod down through the wax with a skewer, to make sure that no air spaces have formed around the wick during shrinkage, and fill the holes with wax. This topping-up procedure may have to be repeated four or five times until the shrinkage is so little that the skewer holding the protruding piece of wick can be removed, the wick pressed down into the soft core, and the final topping-up done.

Leave the candle for several hours or overnight to cool completely, then remove the mould seal; the candle should slide easily from the mould.

With household product containers for moulds, removing the finished candle can sometimes prove difficult and the surface gloss uneven. To overcome this, leave about 152mm (6in) of wick protruding from the base of the mould. Have a kettle of boiling water to hand and, with the length of wick firmly gripped between two fingers, twirl the whole thing while pouring boiling water down the outside of the mould until the candle slides out. To correct any imperfections that may occur on the candle surface, dunk the whole candle into boiling water two or three times, being extremely careful not to wet the wick.

If using a commercially produced mould, difficulties in removing the candle are rare; if it sticks, place the whole thing in the refrigerator for an hour or so, whereupon a sharp clap against the palm of the hand should do the trick.

If the base is not quite even, it may be levelled off with a planing tool, but do not forget to collect the shavings on newspaper, ready for remelting. There is no waste with this hobby. It is quite an added bonus that any initial disasters can be utilised for your ultimate success!

Projects

MARBLED CANDLES

Having had good results with some straightforward one-colour candles, it is only natural to experiment with different effects and designs, and here the easiest one to try is the marbled candle.

Heat a pan of wax until melted and add dye and perfume if required, aiming for a strong not a pastel shade. When ready, pour the wax into a shallow tinfoil freezer tray or a swiss-roll tin and leave it for 20 to 30 minutes. Room temperatures will naturally affect the setting times. Wax, like custard, forms a skin as it cools; when the fingertip can be pressed into the wax yet no liquid wax

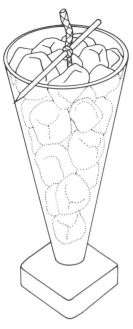

beneath the surface spurts around the fingernail, score the wax across with a knife, as when scoring fudge. Put it aside to cool and harden.

In another pan, put a second batch of colourless wax to melt whilst wicking up and preparing the mould. Then, making certain that the tautened wick stays centralised, break the coloured wax slab along the prepared score lines into fudge-sized chunks and fill the prepared mould to the brim (Fig. 9.6).

When the wax in the pan is ready, just pour the colourless mix over the chunks in the mould. If some chunks protrude above the surface, allow them to soften in the hot wax for a few minutes and then press them down with the point of the wicking needle or a cocktail stick. Shrinkage will occur as before, but not so noticeably, and topping up should be necessary only two or three times.

Slide or untie the wick retainer and finish off the candle as for the one-colour block candles. Polish your candle to give it a gloss, across its surface rather than up or down, with a clean duster.

A mosaic effect is obtained by using multicoloured chips rather than just one shade; a very pale yellow instead of a colourless overpouring wax gives a most attractive and interesting difference in the overall shading.

PERFUMED CANDLES

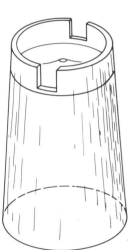

Figures 9.6 & 7

By now the initial successes may inspire you to invest in a commercial mould (Fig. 9.7). Unfortunately perfumed wax cannot be used in these moulds as the perfume in the wax spoils the surface of the mould and thus the finish of the candle. You can get round this problem by perfuming the chunks and leaving the pouring wax odourless.

Perfumes are a must once disasters are a thing of the past and each candle to leave the mould is yet another triumph. Unperfumed candles seem to uninteresting while the range of fragrances is extensive and tempting. A good craft shop carrying a stock of basic candle-making materials and equipment will generally have a selection available. Perfumes come in 14gm ($\frac{1}{2}$oz) bottles, which does not seem very much, but amounts to some four hundred drops.

At 1 drop per 28gm (1oz) of wax it does in fact go a very long way. Maybe the local shop will only carry a small selection—the best-sellers, sandalwood, and a few flowery ones such as rose, jasmin and honeysuckle—but there are twenty-nine perfumes to choose from in essence form alone.

There seems to be no substitute for candle perfume. Oil of citronella may be used successfully, but purely from the experimental angle to see how, or even if, it works.

An unusual, but useful, candle to try, using yellow-dyed wax strongly perfumed with oil of citronella, can be made by using scallop shells as moulds. Fill the shells with the wax and, when it is practically set, after about 20 minutes, insert a 35mm (1$\frac{1}{2}$in) stiffened length of wick in the centre, top up with more molten wax and leave to cool.

In the garden, at a picnic or by the pool, these garden candles burning will not only look attractive, but will also help to keep the midges at bay—pretty and practical!

FLOATING CANDLES

These very simple but effective little candles can be made from all the oddments of waxes from previous candle-making sessions: pairings from levelling bases, old and odd stubs of burnt-out candles, in fact any wax, may be utilised.

All together in the melting pot, the dominant colour will be a shade of brown, which may then be lightened into more autumnal tints, or chrysanthemum colours, by the generous addition of colourless wax. It does not necessarily stop at that. Many unusual shades can be discovered by adding varying amounts of pink or red dyes. The experiments with colour are endless.

Bun tins make excellent moulds, but to make floating flowers, brioche moulds (Fig. 9.8) from a good kitchenware shop are well worth the extra outlay. The 76mm (3 in) diameter across the top are the best size and take about 42.5gm (1½ oz) wax—these will then burn for a good 2 hours or more.

Into a pan of molten wax, dip 30.5cm (1 ft) or so of 25.5mm (1 in) wick, remove it and, when excess wax has stopped dripping from the end, just hook it over the plate rack of your cooker and leave it to solidify. Then cut it into 32mm (1¼ in) lengths. Now, half-fill each bun tin or brioche mould with wax and leave them for 15 minutes or until no liquid wax squirts up around the fingernail when the surface skin is pressed. As centrally as possible insert a piece of wick into the setting wax and, after another 5 minutes, top the mould up to the brim with more molten wax. If the wick tends to topple over, it can easily be coaxed upright with the tip of a cocktail stick, or maybe by snipping the wick shorter by 3mm (⅛ in) or so, to prevent it being top-heavy.

After about 1 hour, you will hear the wax cracking as it shrinks away from the mould and the candle can then be easily lifted out by its wick. Three or four of these little flowers floating in a bowl of water with some greenery make a very attractive and unusual decoration either for the centre of the dining-table or as individual flowers at each place-setting at a party. They can be varied for all occasions—pink or blue for christenings, white for a wedding party or coming-of-age celebration. All colours may be used for a child's birthday party, with no fear of molten wax being spilt on the table.

LAYER CANDLES

This variation on the basic block candle is quite fun to make and only necessitates having different coloured waxes ready for melting.

Wick and prepare the mould; pour in the first layer of molten wax to a depth of 19mm (¾ in). Leave to cool for about 30 minutes. Now, bringing a different coloured wax to its 85°C (185°F) plus temperature, pour in the second layer. Continue in this manner until the mould is filled to the brim (Fig. 9.9). After 1 hour pierce down through the wax with a skewer and fill the shrinkage hole with clear molten wax.

Figures 9.8 & 9

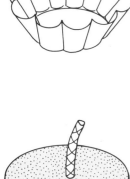

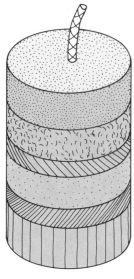

A variation on this design (Fig. 9.10) is to tier the mould slightly; when the first layer of wax is ready to take the second pouring, tilt the mould in the opposite direction, then reverse the tilting angle yet again for the following layers until ready for the final pouring, when the mould should be stood upright so that the base will be flat.

Remember always to pour each layer before the previous one has completely cooled or the layers either will not adhere to each other properly, or, although adhering, a band of bubbles will form over each join, thus spoiling the finished look of the candle.

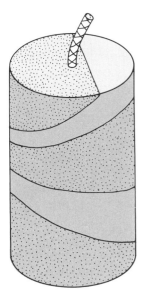

Figure 9.10

APPLIQUE CANDLES

This is a variation on the basic block candle. A culinary decorative art is to take an ordinary leaf, wash it well and dip it into melted chocolate and, when the leaf is peeled away from the setting chocolate, you are left with a perfect facsimile. It is possible to do this in wax; it does not take long to know when the wax is set enough for the leaf to be peeled off without damaging the delicate wax skin that forms.

Have an ordinary household candle burning, a pan of boiling water, a handy cloth and a teaspoon. Take your basic block candle, dip the teaspoon into the boiling water, wipe it dry and, with the back of the hot spoon, soften a spot on the side of the candle; apply a blob of molten wax from the burning candle and quickly, but gently, press your wax leaf into position.

Furnishing braids, especially those containing gold thread, make lovely candle trimmings. Measure round the candle with a tape measure, then cut a length of braid 38 mm ($1\frac{1}{2}$ in) longer than the circumference of the candle; seal the ends against fraying with cellotape, then trim to shape. After deciding where the braid should be placed, stick it into place using a white glue, then, holding a short pin with tweezers, heat it to red-hot, let it cool slightly, then press it through the loose end of the taped braid and into the candle.

ICE CANDLES

You will require one household candle, 0.45 kg (1 lb) wax/stearin mix, colourant, ice cubes and a straight-sided polythene container.

While the wax mix is melting, take some ice cubes. Wrap them in a towel and crush them well with a wooden mallet. Dip the candle tip into the melting wax to waterproof the wick, then holding the candle centrally in the polythene mould, point down, pack it round well with the crushed ice to within 19 mm ($\frac{3}{4}$ in) of the top of the mould. Add required colour to the melting wax and, when it is ready, fill the mould to the brim.

After about 30 minutes, grip the protruding length of candle and gently remove the whole block from the mould; with the breadknife or saw remove the protruding end of the candle so that it is level with the base and stand the block in a bowl or on the draining-board. As the melting ice trickles away, a filigree of wax will become apparent around the centre wax core. When all the ice has gone, stand the candle on a cloth in a warm room for 2 or 3 days to dry out thoroughly before burning.

For a delicate pastel glow, use a vividly coloured centre candle and over the crushed ice pour colourless wax which will take on a tint from the colourful core piece.

WATER CANDLES

These are similar to the ice candle in that a centre core candle is used, but in this case the molten wax is formed into free flowing shapes by water action.

Take a 203 mm (8 in) or 229 mm (9 in) dish—a pie-dish will do—half-fill it with molten wax to which you have ideally added 1% plastic additive. Leave until partially set and then press an ordinary candle into the centre and leave the whole to cool completely.

Heat more wax, fill a bucket three-quarters full with water and stir vigorously. Quickly fill the pie-dish with molten wax and, holding the candle at the tip, plunge it down into the swirling water. Now stir the water in the reverse direction, pour more wax into the pie-dish and repeat the process. The molten wax in both cases will come to the surface of the water, setting into wierd and wonderful swirls around the centre core. Use a white core with red pouring wax to give the effect of flames licking up around the burning candle. Leave for 2 days before lighting.

HURRICANE CANDLES

These candles are very easy to make and have an indefinite life-span. Basically, they are just a shell of wax into which is placed a votive candle or night-light. It is the decoration of the shell which makes each candle a work of art to delight recipients.

To make the shell one needs a large container not less than 102 mm (4 in) diameter, a straight-sided tin can makes a suitable mould, but the rim at the top must be removed with a pair of tin snips, otherwise it will be very difficult to remove the cold shell from the tin.

Fill the tin can to the brim with molten wax, be sure the tin stands level, and leave for 1 hour, after which the wax should be poured out of the can, leaving 6.5–13 mm ($\frac{1}{4}$–$\frac{1}{2}$ in) of setting wax adhering to the sides and base. With the flat of a knife, smooth the insides of the forming shell and leave it to cool and harden. Remove it from the can and, with the blade of the knife, smooth off the line left on the wax by the seam of the can.

Decorating the shell is really the exciting part; all your latent artistry is given free reign, and don't forget disasters can be melted down!

It is possible to paint in oils directly on to candle-wax, free-style if you are an artist, using stencils if not. Dried pressed flowers can be stuck on with white glue, then a light coating of colourless nail varnish brushed gently over the surface for protection. Lace ribbons in horizontal, vertical or oblique lines, paper cut-outs, i.e. the lacy edging from a cake doyley, in fact most ways of

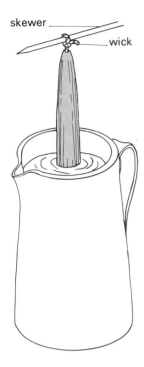

skewer

wick

adding appliqué to the basic block candle as already described, can be applied to the hurricane candle.

DIPPED CANDLES

Tapers as well as dipped candles can be made in various thicknesses, but as a rule most candles are 2.5 cm (1 in) in diameter.

Heat a pan of wax till melted and add dye to the required shade. Take care not to overheat—your temperature, remember, should be 85°C (180°F). Fill a tall jug with wax, taking extreme care not to splash yourself or the cooker with hot wax. Remember it will react like burning fat. To a skewer, tie one end of a suitable length of wick securely and dip the wick into the molten wax. Remove it by pulling it out as straight as you can and holding it out of the wax until it hardens (Fig. 9.11).

Keep dipping in the same way until you get a candle of the required diameter, then hang it up on kitchen cup hooks to dry.

Should your jug of wax cool before you reach the diameter that you want, then you must re-heat the wax to 85°C (180°F) before proceeding with dipping. This, of course, will apply after you have dipped each candle, for the wax will have cooled well below the temperature of 85°C (180°F) before you start on the second candle. As you master this method you will find it easier and less frustrating to do a pair of candles at a time. You need only use a wider jug to accommodate the diameter of two candles with room to spare all round (Fig. 9.12).

ROLLED BEESWAX CANDLES

These are probably the easiest and to some the most beautiful of all candles although, as has been mentioned earlier on, they are expensive when made purely from sheet wax. No heat is required as you will find room temperature will be enough to make the sheet workable; in winter or colder days you might find it necessary to warm the wax near a heater.

Cut a length of the correct size wick for the diameter of the finished candle, but leaving sufficient at one end to take the flame.

Place the wick along one edge of the sheet of beeswax. Fold the edge of the wax over the wick and roll evenly and gently, keeping it level all the time. Finish by pressing the edge evenly and gently to the finished candle so as to prevent it coming adrift. Trim the wick to about 6.5 mm ($\frac{1}{4}$ in) and dip the end in molten beeswax so that it will light (Fig. 9.13).

To vary the candle you can cut the sheet of beeswax at an angle from the top of one end to half-way down the other end. You start rolling, of course, from the longest side and proceed as above (Fig. 9.14 & 15).

Much emphasis has been made on the use of kitchen equipment in candle-making. This has been quite deliberate, because sometimes, a great deterrent to starting a new hobby can be the initial outlay on equipment. Wax is non-toxic and therefore it is not necessary to put aside pots and pans, etc., for

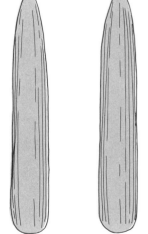

Figures 9.11 & 12

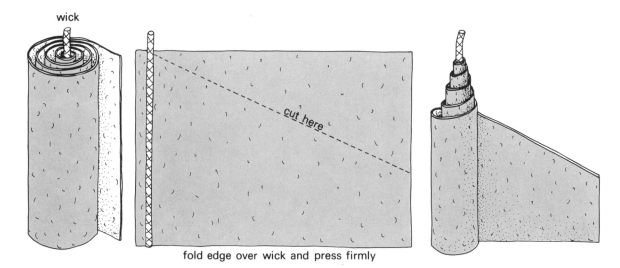

wick

cut here

fold edge over wick and press firmly

Left to right
Figures 9.13–15

specific use. All metal pots and pans, bun tins and trays, can easily be cleaned by placing them upside-down on newspaper in a hot oven for say 30 minutes at gas regulo 7, electricity 218°C (425°F), rinsing quickly with boiling water, and washing up in the usual way. The rest of the equipment, such as the bread-knife, hacksaw, grater, thermometer and strainer, will come clean with having boiling water poured over them, before washing-up.

Glass or metal moulds can also be cleaned by placing them in a hot oven on newspaper for 1 minute or so, then just wiping them over with a dry handy cloth.

THELMA JOHNS

10 Dorset Buttons

HOW LITTLE we consider the humble button. That it has a romantic and fascinating history is something of a surprise to most people and to find that the county of Dorset nurtured the roots of this now worldwide industry is even more surprising.

To begin with, the use of buttons for the common man was unknown. Clothing was simple and coarse, fastened with tapes or pins; even pins were expensive (hence the term 'pin money') so one had to be fairly well off, even for the purchase of a pin to hold on your bonnet. The nun's habit of today was the common dress of the matron of the thirteenth century and these garments have remained the same to the present day; they have no buttons but are fastened with tapes and pins.

The buttons then were usually made by craftsmen and were in gold or silver or other rare metals, sometimes inlaid with enamel or precious stones. These buttons were made as far back as prehistoric times but were marks of rank, badges of office, or just decoration, and had little to do with holding clothing together. Some were found in the tombs of the Pharaohs and in graves of oriental princes.

As merchants of the world travelled further afield and discovered finer fabrics with which to beguile the courts of Europe, the heavy brooch, the pin and tie-string were found to be destructive to the rich and delicate silks, velvets and fine linens, and the button began to be used in its present familiar role. Many were hand-made in horn, wood or bone. All were expensive. Still the ordinary man used the pin and tie-string; homespun was the only cloth he could afford anyway.

The history of button-making most certainly pre-dates the Dark Ages, for we know many beautiful examples are to be seen in antiquarian museums throughout the world. Prior to the invention of the button, clothes were fastened with pins, brooches, ties, buckles and sashes. Then came the toggle-type button, made of horn passed through a loop to secure the garment. By the middle of the fourteenth century, long rows of buttons on clothes were to be seen in Italy and became so popular that two cities, Florence and Lucca, passed a law which forbade servant girls to wear buttoned sleeves above the elbows. Failure to observe this law was punishable by the poor girl being whipped naked through the streets.

Buttons were also worn as ornaments from about the middle of the sixteenth century. Those wishing to be dressed in the extreme of fashion, displayed a veritable wealth of them on their clothes, whether useful or just decorative did not matter. Hence, many religious bodies forbid the use of buttons and will only allow hooks and eyes. We count the buttons on our coats to the old rhyme:

Rich man, poor man, beggar-man, thief,
Doctor, lawyer, merchant, chief.

Some buttons which appeared to be only ornaments had a very definite use, such as the ones on men's coat-sleeves, which served to fasten back the sleeves in order that the hands might remain free, and at the back of the frock-coat, to button-up the long skirts of the coat when riding horseback.

At first buttons were very expensive, being made of gold, silver or pearl and ornamented with enamels and precious stones. They were shaped and decorated by skilled craftsmen, working on one button at a time. Many other materials are used today, ranging from shells and ivory, bone and horn, to glass, porcelain, leather, plastic and paperboard. Others are covered in all kinds of cloth and many are not sewn on but simply have a shank, which passes through a spring-clip on the other side. Birmingham is the chief centre of button-making in England.

Materials and equipment

rust-proof brass rings—various sizes	fine button-hole thread
rust-proof small stainless steel washers	metallic threads
wooden rings	string
strips and small squares of white, cream or beige cotton	raffia
white and coloured sewing cotton	fine sewing needles
crochet cotton	crewel needle
	nail file
	scissors

RINGS AND WASHERS

Care must be taken in purchasing the rings or washers as bases for any of these buttons. Any metal should be rust-proof; brass is by far the best, but tiny stainless steel rings can be purchased from fishing tackle shops. The hunt for rings and bases is a hobby in itself and one finds oneself always with an eye open for another source of supply. The best way to buy curtain rings is by the boxful; they are much cheaper that way. Prepared rings are very expensive, but one can sometimes find unusual sizes packed in this way, especially the larger ones. It is also worth asking precision engineers—some of their off-cuts can be most useful and if asked they might even make up a few of unusual sizes for you.

Generally speaking, the plastic and nylon rings are not suitable; they are too flexible and the plastic ones tend to break. Wooden rings may be used to make larger buttons; in fact some of the Bird's-Eyes made after 1900, during the attempted revival of button-making in Dorset, were made on conventional wooden button-moulds without the cloth-winding process described later.

THREADS

A good thread to start with is crochet cotton, as it is strong and supple. This can be bought by the ball from most good haberdashers or craft needlework shops, and there are some exciting colours and textures. As I will describe in detail, one can produce very interesting buttons by changing the thread colours at various stages in the manufacture of the button and, just as it becomes a hobby to look for rings of various sizes, so also the search for unusual thread is fascinating.

Colours can be varied in wool as in other threads. The Crosswheel, for example, can also be made in wool, but must be more carefully washed. Buttons for other garments may be made up in any manner of thread, even thread pulled from the fabric can be used if it is firm enough.

NEEDLES

It is best to use a crewel needle with a large eye; a needle with a point can inflict painful injury to the fingers and result in blood-stained buttons.

Basic Techniques

A hundred years have passed since the sudden death of the Dorset Button industry, but we are indeed fortunate that some examples of these unique buttons have been preserved. The very fineness of the work and the minute size of some of them makes it very difficult to make accurate copies. However, some can be made with a certain degree of accuracy—with others, such as the Dorset Knob (Fig. 10.1), reputed to be the oldest design of Dorset button, one can merely speculate as to the method of manufacture. Nothing is known of any special use, perhaps it was a general all-purpose button—certainly it was one of the most popular, and now the most rare.

The second in this category is the High Top (Fig. 10.2), originally used on the waistcoats of fine gentlemen, the kind of waistcoat that, in fact, went from neck to knee. These garments would have had numerous buttons down the front, fastened through loops by a servant armed with a button-hook. In addition, these waistcoats were thickly embroidered and quilted and had many High Top buttons used in the decoration.

The Dorset Buttons described, however, can be made with greater certainty.

THE SINGLETON

First, cut a small square of cloth, then cut off the corners to make a rough circle (Fig. 10.3)—the corners are retained as packing for the inside of the

Figures 10.1 & 2

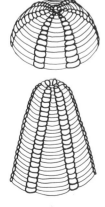

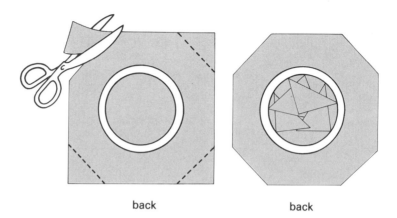

back   back

Left to right
Figures 10.3 & 4
Below
Figures 10.5-7

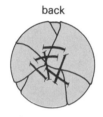

back

front

button. Place the ring in the centre of the cloth and place the scraps in the middle of the ring (Fig. 10.4). Then fold the ends to the centre and secure them with a few stitches (Fig. 10.5). Now turn over the packed ring and work closely either to the outside edge with tiny back-stitch (Fig. 10.6), or over the edge with blanket-stitch. Then work four or five french knots in the middle and the button is finished (Fig. 10.7).

The Singleton can be made on quite a large ring and may take the place of more conventional covered buttons and is much more substantial. Covered buttons do tend to fall to pieces in the wash or at the cleaners, or disintegrate at most inconvenient moments. These buttons can also be used when deep-buttoning small dainty items such as baby-clothes. They look exquisite if made in silk or satin, even nylon, and used on nightdresses, housecoats, underwear or evening dresses. Needless to say, these buttons are particularly suitable for children's dresses; even fine denim looks very well made up into Singletons, especially if the stitching is in a contrasting colour with perhaps some embroidery in the centre instead of a flower or french knots.

Yet again, they can be used for decorative purposes only: in any embroidery or collage, to decorate collars, to edge cuffs, or to accentuate tucks or mock pockets. They also look really attractive on hand-made silk lampshades.

THE BIRD'S-EYE

This also consists of a ring similar to the one used as a base for the Singleton. This time bind it tightly with a thin strip of material until the ring is nearly filled to the centre. Then blanket-stitch around and over the ring, from the centre to the outside, leaving the ridge of the stitch in a neat ring on the outside edge and the face of the button flat (Fig. 10.8). To achieve a more finished result, place the face of the completed button on a hard surface, such as the bottom of a plate, and press the ridge of stitches towards the plate with a small blunt blade—the handle end of a nail file is ideal.

These dainty little buttons have many uses in the modern world. They can be made small enough to use on baby clothes, being very soft and light, thus making them especially suitable.

Figure 10.8

Variations can be made using coloured thread and small washers as a base instead of curtain rings. Larger buttons can be produced for use on hand-knitted jumpers or any garment you might make, although, on the whole, these buttons look better on simple garments, such as smocks and cotton blouses.

THE OLD DORSET

This is one old button that can be made with complete accuracy, apart from the fact that, these days, cotton instead of linen is more generally used.

Select the ring you require. Holding it in the left hand, button-hole-stitch over and around the ring closely and evenly with any chosen thread, working from left to right and with an upward movement—this is known as 'casting' (Fig. 10.9 & 10). The little knots that appear at the outside of the ring are now pushed to the back—a procedure known as 'slicking' (Fig. 10.11). For the next stage or 'laying', a long length of thread is taken, joined to the ring, and wound down the back and across the centre of the ring to the opposite side, then up the front to the top again. The second winding will be slightly to the left of the first at the top and to the right at the bottom (Fig. 10.12). Continue this process evenly and closely, turning the ring slightly as every thread is laid until it is completely covered. Thread a fine needle with the remaining end and begin the final process of 'rounding'.

Make a cross, i.e. one stitch each way, in the exact centre to catch the threads together. Then carry up the thread immediately under the ring to the outside edge. Take up the threads forming the 'spokes' in pairs—thus each thread in front is taken up with the corresponding thread behind—and back-stitch all around the inside edge twice. To do this, bring the thread through in front of, and then back over, one of the spokes. Catching in the back thread of the spoke and turning the ring to the left, bring the thread through to the front of the next spoke and then back over it, thereby making another back-stitch. Continue around the inside edge of the ring for two circuits and anchor the thread with a few stitches into the threadwork on the back of the button (Fig. 10.13).

Other variations of the Old Dorset can be achieved by carrying out the rounding in the centre with a contrasting thread. Another method is to repeat the rounding on top of the back-stitch with two rows of chain-stitch. This gives

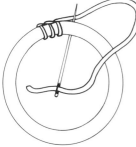

Above
Figures 10.9 & 10
Left to right
Figures 10.11–13

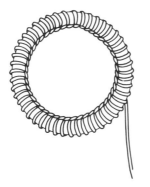
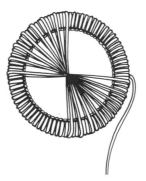
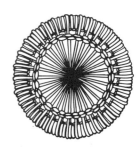

a most attractive and rather more sophisticated finish to this otherwise rather rustic button. Indeed their original use was exceedingly rustic, being the ideal button for the linen smocks of the village tradesmen and farmers. Even more sophisticated would be a few french knots or daisy-stitches embroidered in the centre of the finished button.

These buttons may be made in any size but look best about the size of a new penny, i.e. 2 cm (0.8 in). Ordinary sewing thread may be used in any colour you wish. Natural or unbleached linen was the original colour, so cream or beige tends to look best. There are some very firm button-hole threads on the market and these provide a rather more chunky button; anything coarser is not suitable.

THE BLANDFORD CARTWHEEL

This button is a very close relative of the Old Dorset and sometimes known as the Crosswheel. The method of construction is similar.

As in the Old Dorset, hold the ring in the left hand and commence the casting. Remember to pull the button-hole-stitch very tightly round the ring, otherwise you may find that the spokes of the wheel will slip round when you come to lay them in place. The little knots created by the button-hole-stitch must be firmly

Figures 10.14–16

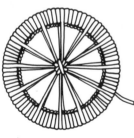

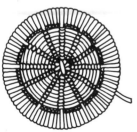

slicked or pushed to the back of the ring, as in the making of the Old Dorset. From this point there is a variation. Proceed with the laying as for the Old Dorset but leave sufficient space between each thread to allow for at least five threads going across the front of the button and five across the back (Fig. 10.14). Take the needle and thread to the centre of the button and make a few stitches from the back to the front, as if you were sewing the button to a garment; this will hold the spokes firmly in position. Make sure that you have caught the threads that cross the back of the button into these central threads (Fig. 10.15). The rounding work on the Cartwheel is done from the centre outwards, not as in the case of the Old Dorset, which is just around the edge. Starting in the centre and from the back, bring the thread through and back-stitch around the spokes, until the whole of the ring is filled right to the inside edge (Fig. 10.16). Finish off by taking the thread through the stitches on the back to the centre again and working a few stitches. This gives a slightly proud centre on the back of the ring, making sewing on easier.

All Dorset Buttons are applied to garments by stitching into the back of the button and in through the cloth of the garment. Cartwheels and Old Dorsets can be stitched on in a similar manner to modern buttons by using matching thread and stitching through the centre of the button. This can sometimes make the centre a little bulky especially on fine buttons.

The Cartwheel can be varied in a number of ways, most commonly by changing the colour of the threads at different stages in the making of the button. For instance, the casting can be done in blue, the laying in white and the rounding in red, giving a most attractive button with a blue border interspersed with white where the laying threads cross the ring, red where the

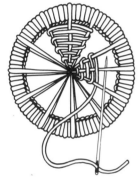

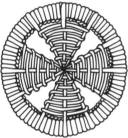

Above
Figures 10.17–19

Below
Figure 10.20

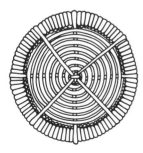

rounding thread covers the white spokes and white again in the centre where the spokes join. Two or three colours can be used during rounding, giving a Catherine wheel appearance, and, in very large buttons, many colours can be used. Very striking results may be produced by using really up-to-date thread such as silver, gold and other metallic yarns. These buttons are most suitable for evening wear.

There is a variation to this button that is said to be the true Crosswheel. This may be so. Certainly the variation forms a Maltese Cross in the centre of the button, but button-workers from the revival of the craft early in this century called both varieties Crosswheel and Cartwheel, so perhaps there were regional differences in naming. For the purpose of identification, we will call this variation the Crosswheel.

THE CROSSWHEEL

Cast in the usual manner (Fig. 10.17). For the best effect a ring 22mm ($\frac{7}{8}$ in) in diameter or over is best. Then lay the spokes, remembering that there must be six threads crossing the ring for this pattern. The laying is centralised as before, but it is best to create a rather thicker centre by stitching in and out of each spoke in turn until a multiple cross is formed right in the centre. The Maltese Cross is formed by working the spokes in threes (Fig. 10.18), rather than round and round as for the Cartwheel.

Starting from the centre, take one set of three threads radiating from the centre, bring the needle and thread from the back and down again to the back, over the thread to the right, then back up in the same place as you started; then down again over the thread to the right—this is a figure-of-eight movement rather than the back-stitch used before. Work these three spokes in the same manner until the inside edge of the ring is reached, taking care not to pull the threads too tightly. As the inside edge of the ring is reached, allow the natural splay of the spokes to remain—this forms one section of the cross. Now start again in the centre of the button and work the next three spokes in the same manner, keeping the tension on the thread the same as for the previously worked section. Continue in the same manner until the central spokes have been divided into four sections, thus forming a cross (Fig. 10.19).

These buttons are most effective if made in a contrasting colour to the fabric of the garment they are to be used on, as the fabric colour shows through the gaps in the spokes. Different coloured threads may be used for each section and also for the casting and laying, producing a harlequin effect.

THE BASKET

Another variation (Fig. 10.20) of the Cartwheel, this type is not often used as a true button, as it is not so firm as the others, but it is useful when extremely coarse yarn such as string or raffia is used. It is also quicker to do.

Commence as before with casting and laying; as with the Crosswheel, six movements across the diameter of the ring can be made, but it is possible to use many more on a large ring. Again start the rounding from the centre of the button, but, in this instance, instead of using a back-stitch, use an under and over stitch in a weaving movement. Bring the needle from the back and, working to the left, go over a spoke and under a spoke as if you were darning, until the edge of the ring is reached. Once more, variations in colour can be used and a lazy daisy embroidered in the centre looks charming and helps to keep the button firm. This pattern, made on a wooden or wicker ring in raffia, can be used as the bottom or lid of a basket or box.

Just one trick of the trade and a few tips. A more definite spoke can be made by laying two or more threads instead of one for each spoke. Once you have mastered the craft with one thread for each spoke—and remember that this means one thread at the front of the ring and one thread at the back, both to be caught together to form one spoke, try two threads for each spoke, two at the front, two at the back, therefore catching four threads together to form one spoke. This sounds a little awesome, but it is worth the extra work especially on larger buttons.

Remember to keep all threads as tight as possible, except in the case of the forming of the cross in the Crosswheel, where they should be firm but not too tight or the cross-shape will not be correctly formed. Provided these buttons have been tightly and securely made, they will wash and wear extremely well, often outliving the garment for which they were made. It is worth removing them from worn-out or discarded garments to store and use again.

Now having mastered the ancient craft of buttony, the door is open to a whole new field of imaginative uses.

First, there is the obvious and traditional use as a button to fasten clothing. The old type, such as Bird's-Eyes and Singletons are small, and would therefore best be used on children's clothing, although I have seen Singletons, made in fine silk or lawn, used on wedding dresses, and they do look very pretty indeed.

Bird's-Eyes are very soft and would be ideal for babies' nightdresses and other tiny garments that fasten at the back. Being so soft, it is best to provide stitched loops rather than button-holes for these delightful little buttons. They were used on the baby-clothes of Napoleon Bonaparte and are sometimes on display in the Louvre Gallery in Paris.

The Old Dorset has many uses as it was traditionally used on the old-style smocks. It is equally attractive on the modern smocks and embroidered blouses, now so popular and fashionable. It is very light and strong and will not pull fine fabrics. Also, being made of thread, it is not slippery and will not slide out of the button-holes of soft fine fabrics as do plastic buttons.

If you do not make your own garments, it is a good idea to change the buttons for your own hand-made ones; this gives the garment a more exclusive look.

These old-style buttons also have uses quite apart from a fastening device. I have seen a delightful collage of a girl collecting apples; all the apples were Bird's-Eyes worked in red, green and yellow. Bird's-Eyes can be used in embroidery as bird's eyes, or any animal's eyes for that matter. They can be worked into contemporary designs, appliqué work or quilting, as the buttons when deep-buttoning the top of a workbox or baby-basket, joined together to make collars, belts, cuffs and, most traditional of all, incorporated into lace as part of the design, or as a fastener. Nothing looks worse than a beautiful lace collar fastened with a plastic or even a pearl button.

The uses to which the Blandford Cartwheel can be put are many and exciting. First let us consider their practical use. The fact that they are strong and light is something that they have in common with all the Dorset Buttons, but this is a quality lacking in many of the buttons we buy today. Provided the thread is of fast colour, they can be boiled and beaten about in the washing-machines and dryers. They can be dry-cleaned with safety, even put through a wringer without splitting, so long as they are kept flat. The iron won't melt them and they will not go soft and sticky and lose their colour. When used on a woollen garment, they will not sag or pull the buttonholes out of shape, in fact they can be made from the same wool as the garment and they will not shrink in washing. They look especially good made up in Arran wool and it is always difficult to find a good button suitable to match this wool or other chunky knits.

There are various other crafts to which button-making can be allied, macramé and basket-making for instance. Buttons made of string or raffia can be used instead of the wooden beads as spacers in macramé work. They can be joined together to add interest to the hanging strings for flower-pot holders and large rings can be worked in the basket-style to form bases for plant pots to stand on if a solid base is needed.

As one works with Dorset Buttons and starts to think of them not just as a button, but as an art form, the possibilities continue to present themselves.

Projects

TABLE-MAT

Very pleasing table-mats can be produced by making a number of quite large, say 51 mm (2 in) buttons, and linking them together. Coarse crochet thread is very suitable for this, as the colours are generally fast and therefore the table-mats can be washed. It is not always necessary to work all the rings into completed buttons; some can be left at the casting stage and interspersed with completed buttons.

The joining of the buttons is a simple operation carried out as follows: place two buttons side by side, thread a needle with the same yarn as they are made from and, starting from the back of the button, push the needle through the threadwork of the spokes just inside the ring and down through the thread-work of the other button, again just inside the ring. Repeat this action three or four times, then take the needle between the buttons outside the rings, and simply wrap the thread over and under the stitches just made two or three times, and finish off by putting a couple of stitches through the threads at the back (Fig. 10.21). This gives a firm join and, by this method, as many buttons can be joined together as you please, either completed buttons, or some complete and some rings with just the casting done.

Figure 10.21

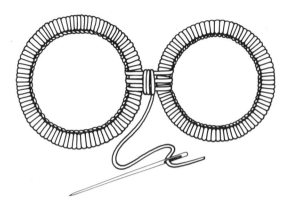

JEWELLERY

All you need to make most attractive earrings is any good waterproof glue and ready-made metal bases that can be obtained from many craft shops. Just one button can be stuck on to the base, or several of varying sizes joined together to form dangling earrings. They also look very smart made with one of the metallic threads. It was sometimes the practice of the later button-makers in Dorset to make buttons spangled with tiny beads, and these were indeed called 'spangles'. This was done by threading the beads on to the thread during the rounding process. Spangles can be used to very good effect in jewellery-making, but I think that the beads destroy the wheel effect; nevertheless, they do look very pretty.

Necklaces and bracelets can be made by simply sewing buttons together to the required length, with hooks and eyes for fasteners. For larger items, such as belts, large hooks and eyes can be disguised by covering them with casting stitch as used on the button rings.

CUFF LINKS

These are perhaps the most popular and can be made in club colours or just to match the shirt, being so cheap to make it is possible to have a set for each shirt. An even cheaper way of producing cuff links, is to link them together with a crochet chain, or even stitch a small piece of metal chain between two buttons. Care must be taken though to use rust-proof chain.

EVENING BAG

One of the prettiest ways of using buttons is to make a most glamorous evening bag. All you have to do is to fasten the buttons together and back them with fabric in a contrasting colour, then stitch the whole thing to a clip. You can find Victorian purse-clips at quite reasonable prices where the original bag has disintegrated or is in bad condition, or a simple envelope shape looks very smart.

Imagination will give you many ideas as to what you can make. If you have endless patience and a good deal of time, very unusual door-curtains or room-dividers can be made by stringing buttons together in matching or contrasting colours. Fire-screens made with bamboo and strings of Dorset Buttons stretched across the frame look most attractive.

Small buttons fastened together look charming as insertions on skirts and blouses; they could even be used as panels in crochet bedspreads, though a complete bedspread made of them would be far too heavy.

The possibilities are endless, but as you enjoy this old craft of Dorset buttony, remember the folk of Dorset, making buttons by the thousand for their livelihood so many years ago.

DIANE MILLER

11

Pressed Flowers

PRESSING FLOWERS is an art with a long but rather vague history. No one seems quite certain as to when it was first done. The earliest reference which I have come across is Hilda R. Robinson's *Pressed Plants as an Art* in which she mentions that an Italian professor of medicine in the sixteenth century pressed herbs for his students to use in their studies.

As an art form, however, it seems to have been most popular during the Victorian age, during which time ladies of society had a great deal of leisure. It was, therefore, not surprising that they should take up many of the rather more refined and sophisticated crafts. There are many delicate and outstanding examples of Victorian pressed flower pictures, which harmonised so well with the elegant surroundings of the times.

Some examples of pressed seaweed are to be found in museums and private collections, but seaweed proved to be an unsuitable plant for pressing, due to the long and complicated process of drying. So, as enthusiasm for seaweed-pressing waned, the more technically simple pressed flower picture gained in popularity.

However, with the end of the Victorian era and the emergence of twentieth-century industrial life, these intricate and delightful flower pictures seemed to disappear in Britain, in common with much of the more gracious side of life. Now, happily, people are beginning to take an interest in this delightful art once again.

Pressing flowers is a means of preserving the beauty of nature, so that it may be enjoyed the whole year round.

In the following pages, you will be given some indication of the pleasure and interest to be gained in learning, through trial and error, the art and joy of flower-pressing.

Materials and equipment

flower-press or telephone directory
pocket flower-press
heavy weight, 4.5 kg (10 lb) or over
tissue paper

blotting paper
newspaper
transparent adhesive plastic
    sheeting

mounting materials	paper and plastic bags
frames	polythene box
glue stick	sharp pair of scissors
tweezers	penknife
small paint-brush	flowers, leaves and grasses

COLLECTING FLOWERS

Before you collect flowers for pressing—consider the plants. Do not overpick. Leave some for other people to see and enjoy. The primrose is a plant that has suffered much over the last few years from being abused. Propagated by seed, and not through its roots, every flower picked means the loss of dozens of seeds and, as a result, the sad depletion of the species. Therefore, conserve them by your thought and awareness and take no more than you require at any one time. Never cut branches from trees or shrubs so as to spoil the look of them.

Collecting material for pressing is both fascinating and totally absorbing. A wealth of colour, and hundreds of different flowers to choose from at any time of the year, will make your walk in the garden or country both rewarding and educational. It is essential that collection is carried out on a dry and sunny day: mid-day or early afternoon is the best time so as to ensure no dew is present. If moisture is present when the material is pressed, not only will the flowers turn brown and lose every vestige of their original colour, but also they will become mouldy.

Before you set out to collect, there are a few things you will need to take along with you, such as paper and plastic bags in which to place your specimens. If you are going to be some time and you pick a bunch of plants, then a dock leaf wrapped around the stems will help to keep them fresh until you return home. You may find, on a very warm day, that certain delicate flowers will wilt very quickly, so it is a good idea to have with you a polythene box lined with newspaper or other absorbent material in which to place them. Do not leave the flowers in the box for more than a couple of hours, however, as moisture may collect on the inside of the lid and ruin them. A sharp pair of scissors or penknife is necessary in your collecting kit, as some stems are quite difficult to break and, if great care is not taken, then the plant itself may be damaged or, worse still, uprooted.

Summer, of course, is generally the best time for collecting as the long days are usually warm and dry but, naturally, there is always much material available during the other seasons of the year, even during the winter months.

Spring is the time for Primroses and the delicate young leaves, just emerging from the buds on the trees. Also the early grasses, such as Wood Melick Grass, can be found.

Summer gives us Buttercups and Daisies and the more mature leaves on the trees, together with a wide range of exquisitely tinted and flowering grasses.

With autumn come the Heathers and brightly coloured flowers of the garden, such as Montbretia, as well as the 'flaming' leaves of the trees and shrubs. There are not so many grasses, but the Common Reed growing by the river, still in its budded, black-purple state, has a lovely flowing appearance in contrast to its spear-like leaves.

What can we find in winter? This is the season for infinite varieties of lichens and mosses and skeleton leaves and dead ghost-like grasses can be seen everywhere.

So you see, each season has an abundance of grasses and flowers to be collected, pressed and framed, used to decorate cards, lampshades, boxes, or for any other purpose that you may devise.

The following list gives the flowers, leaves, grasses, and other plants that I have found to be the most useful and perfect, regarding shape and consistency of colour retention:

Apple blossom. The bud is best used. Colour turns to a very delicate beige from white or pink.

Asparagus foliage. Very delicate and fern-like, presses well.

Bird's Foot Trefoil. Found growing almost anywhere from June to August. Retains its colour well.

Broom. Press the individual florets of this late summer-flowering bush. Retains its colour well.

Buttercup. There is a wide variety of these bright yellow flowers, nearly all flowering from April through to September. Colour retention is very good.

Carrot foliage. Presses well and has a useful shape.

Celandine. A very common wild flower and garden weed. Flowers appear as early as February through until April. Press the whole heads. Does not retain colour for long, but turns to an attractive pale cream.

Clematis montana. A late summer-flowering, wall-climbing, garden shrub. Press either, the whole head, or individual petals. Colour turns to a warm brown.

Clover. Pink or White. Found growing abundantly in fields, from May to September. A heavy press is required here. A certain amount of colour is lost, but material is useful for collages. The leaves can also be pressed.

Common Bent Grass. A very delicate grass, flowering almost anywhere from June to August.

Cornflower. Grows wild during June to August in cornfields, but cultivated varieties are very common in gardens. Press the petals only. Colour retention is good.

Cow Parsley. This and its relatives are found anywhere from April onwards. It is a very delicate flower when pressed, a pleasant combination of green and cream.

Daffodil. Wild or cultivated types can be used. Colour retention is good, but the flower must be dismembered before pressing.

Dahlia. Press the individual petals of the dark-coloured flowers. Retains colour very well.

Daisy. Those with the pink tinge to the edge of the petals are especially attractive. Retains the whiteness well.

Delphinium. Press the individual florets of this late summer-flowering garden plant. Retains its colour very well.

Ferns. The mature leaves retain their greenness better than the verdant young leaves.

Forget-me-nots. Delightfully delicate. Press either individual florets or whole sprays. Retains colour well.

French Marigold. Press the individual petals. Colour stays well. Autumn-flowering annuals.

Fuchsia. The small dark varieties are best. Autumn-flowering. Heavy press required. Colour retention very good.

Golden Rod. Autumnal garden flower. Press sprays as required under a heavy press. Good colour retention.

Heartsease (*Field or Wild Pansy*). These delightful miniature pansies are found growing wild and in gardens at any time from April to October. They retain their colour well for a short while.

Heather. All varieties, both cultivated and wild, are useful. A heavy press is required. Colours are retained well.

Herb Robert. The red leaves of this plant, found mainly in the autumn, are probably more useful than the flowers themselves, as these tend to become transparent.

Honeysuckle. This beautifully perfumed climbing plant flowers from June through to September. When pressed it generally turns to varying shades of brown and beige, depending on whether the florets are still budded or open. Remove the individual florets for pressing. This is one of my main standby's.

Hydrangea. Press the individual florets of this late summer-flowering shrub. Retains colour well and produces delightful pastel shades.

Lady's Bedstraw. Found during the months July to September, especially on chalky hillsides. Goes very dark when pressed, sometimes almost black.

Limanthese (*Poached Egg Plant*). Border plant, summer-flowering. Retains colour well.

Lobelia. Summer- and autumn-flowering annual. Retains colour well.

Maple leaves. Press at any time of the year.

Meadow Cranesbill. Blooms from June to September. Loses some colour during pressing, but this usually blends well with the colour that remains. Pleasant shape.

Mimosa. A spring-flowering shrub or tree. Press whole sprays, depending on requirements. A lovely yellow when pressed.

Monbretia. These bright orange, autumn-flowering perennials retain their colour well. Press individual flowers and buds.

Old Man's Beard. Press when in its seeded state. Found during late autumn.

Ox-eye Daisy. Found especially in meadows during June to August. Press the individual petals.

Pansy. Press the whole flower. Colour does not stay for very long.

Poppies. Press the petals only. The common Red Poppy is found from June to September and colour retention is good. The Welsh or Yellow Poppy is found mostly in south-west England and Wales, but does turn up here and there in gardens in other parts of the country. The colour turns an attractive amber. The large garden poppy is also good to press.

Primrose. Flowers as early as February through until May. Retains colour well.

Quaking Grass. Found generally on hillsides, flowering from June to August. Press it before and after the seed heads have spread. The cultivated variety can also be used, but is not so delicate and needs a heavy press.

Saxifrage. Both pink and white varieties can be pressed. Found blooming in many gardens during April and May. Retains colour well.

Silverweed. Flowers and leaves are both good for pressing. Found on waste-ground and roadsides especially. Flowers from July to August. Flower colour stays well and leaves are a delicate green.

Spindle Leaves. Best pressed in the autumn for the beautiful red and orange colours.

Sunflower. Press the individual petals of this universally known and loved flower. Retains its colour well.

Virginia Creeper. Press these leaves at any time of the year.

Wallflower. Pressed mainly for the lovely rich colours of this summer-flowering garden annual. Press the individual petals. Colour retention is excellent.

Wild Rose. Press just the petals. This flower, that seems to represent the English summer, provides us with a wide variety of pastel shades. The texture of the pressed petals is like that of very fine velvet.

Willow Herb (*also Rose-Bay*). Grows near streams and in ditches from July to September. Found in woodland clearings especially. Press individual florets. Colour retention good for a short while.

Wood Melick Grass. As indicated by its name, found generally in and around woodlands. The grass blades and the flowering seed heads press well. Flowers during April and May.

Wood Millet Grass. Flowers from May to July. Also a woodland grass. Has a lovely flow to it and the colour is a delicate green.

Wood Sorrel. Press the leaves only.

Yarrow. A very common wild plant. Press only the foliage which is an unusual shape.

Yellow Alyssum. Spring-flowering garden plant. Press the whole head. Retains colour well for a short while.

There are, of course, many other plants that can be pressed, not mentioned here, but these are for you to discover. This list is merely a guideline for the uninitiated, based on the materials that I prefer and work best with.

EQUIPMENT FOR PRESSING

The minimum amount of equipment is required for this most pleasurable of pastimes. The cost is negligible; therefore, anyone with time to spare may

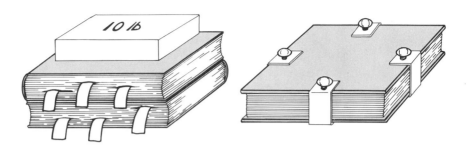

Left to right
Figures 11.1 & 2

indulge in pressing flowers. Your first requirement is, of course, a flower-press. This can be either a bought one or a home-made one designed exclusively for the purpose. You can use a large book with absorbent pages—old telephone directories are excellent. A heavy weight is needed to place on top of the book; a breeze block is ideal, but anything weighing more than 4.5 kg (10 lb) would be adequate (Fig. 11.1). Other requirements are just tissue paper, or tissues, blotting or newspaper, and a dry airy room in which to store the books once the flowers are placed between the leaves.

Should you prefer to use a flower-press instead of books, all you need to make one are: two pieces of hardboard or plywood about 30 cm (12 in) square, between which you need to place sheets of blotting paper and newspaper arranged alternately, and four small clamps to hold the press together and to exert the necessary pressure (Fig. 11.2).

Figure 11.3

A smaller version of this press about 7.5 or 10 cm (3 or 4 in) square to carry in a pocket, may be made in exactly the same way, only instead of clamps, four strong elastic bands can be used (Fig. 11.3).

Basic techniques

PRESSING

When you have the material you wish to press, proceed as follows:

Using an old telephone directory, open the book at the centre. Place an absorbent tissue on the right-hand page and on to the tissue arrange the specimens to be pressed, making sure that they do not touch each other.

Now very carefully cover the flowers, etc., with another tissue, place a tab with the names of the specimens and date of pressing in the book (Fig. 11.4), and close extremely carefully, making sure all the flowers are still in position.

Next, open the book at a stage half-way between the centre and one of the covers and repeat the pressing sequence once again.

The thicker the book, the more you will be able to get into it. When you have finished filling the book with sufficient flowers and leaves, buds and stalks, etc., place it on a flat surface, putting your breeze block, or whatever weight you wish to use, on the centre of the closed book. As more books are filled, build them up, one on top of the other, placing the newest book at the bottom and ending with the additional weight on top.

When using a flower-press specifically designed for the purpose, first place

Figure 11.4

a layer of folded newspaper on the bottom piece of hardboard, followed by a layer of blotting or tissue paper. Next, lay on the material to be used and cover with another layer of tissue or blotting paper, then another layer of folded newspaper. Repeat the process again with the blotting paper, and so on, until the press is full. Finally, screw the clamps down tightly.

It is a good idea, when pressing a particular flower for the first time, to test its qualities for colour retention by leaving it in direct sunlight for a day or two. Should there be a noticeable amount of fade, then use it only on cards, unless the 'new' colour is useful in a picture. You will find that some flowers are worth pressing for their shape alone, even though the colour may fade.

The material being pressed should be left for at least 6 weeks before being used. The tissue should be changed after 2 or 3 weeks when the material is rather lush. Once pressed, the samples can be removed and stored in large books until ready for use, thus leaving the pressing books, or press, available for further material.

DESIGN

One cannot or perhaps should not, influence anyone regarding designs. It is much better that you should experiment with colour, texture and lay-out and obtain the satisfaction of completing the work yourself. This is particularly so where pressed flowers are concerned and, like any other art, once you have the materials to hand, it is entirely up to you what you do with them.

There are, however, one or two rudimentary points to consider and observe when designing. First of all, it is most important not to overcrowd your 'canvas'. Anyone can fill an empty working surface with as many flowers as they can possibly get into it, and this would show a complete lack of subtlety. Spaces are as important as the flowers themselves, helping to enhance the shape and colour of the finished picture.

When designing, it is probably simpler to place the pressed plants which you intend using on the material that will eventually form the background. Move the pieces of flowers, stalks and leaves around, until you feel that the balance is correct and the overall picture attractive. Have tweezers and a small paint-brush near you; they will help in moving delicate specimens. A pair of fine scissors will be needed to cut away unwanted stalks or parts of ragged flower petals and leaves.

There are many types of material to which you can attach pressed flowers, for example, cartridge paper, card, velvet or silk. When fixing your design to the chosen material, use just the amount of glue necessary to hold it in place. A glue stick is very easy to use but, with careful handling and a delicate touch, any glue may be used with confidence.

MOUNTING

Having glued all the pieces in place, you may wish to frame the design. If glass is to be used, then you must cover the picture as soon as possible, so that moisture in the air does not affect the dried material. Greeting cards, book-marks, note-pads or gift-tags should be covered with transparent adhesive plastic sheeting. Designs for small items, such as gift-tags, should be made with one or two little florets and small stems, and the tiniest leaves or buds. Leave enough room for any written message you wish to write, then cover the flowers with a small piece of the transparent adhesive plastic. Plain transparent perspex finger-plates are available from good hardware stores and these may be placed over a mounted design, cut to the size of the plate. The finger-plate should have the screw-holes already drilled through it, so mark and punch corresponding holes on the card before attempting to fasten the completed finger-plate to the door.

Projects

GIFT-TAGS

This is a very easy project to begin with as all you require on the card is a design made up from one or two simple flowers from the following list, or from any other flowers, leaves and grasses indigenous to your country:

Orange: French Marigold, foliage—young Yarrow.
Green: Virginia Creeper.
Mauve: Hydrangea and young Yarrow leaves.
Yellow: Buttercup and buds, foliage made up from Carrot leaves.
Red: Fuchsia—reassembled after initially pressing separately.

Cover the design with transparent adhesive plastic.

A FRIEZE

A frieze with a pressed flower design is a most effective way of brightening a plain wall. Arrange the flowers on a long strip of transparent plastic adhesive sheeting and attach it directly to the wall.

BOOK OF PRESSED FLOWERS

A most welcome and attractive present would be a book of pressed flower designs. There are so many themes to use for a friend who delights in flowers: the seasons, favourite flowers, or flowers from a particular place, bringing back memories of happy days spent in your garden or countryside.

LAMPSHADES

The tube lampshade is by far the easiest type to decorate with flowers, leaves or grasses, as you only need to arrange the design, then either cover it with transparent sheeting or simply lacquer over the flowers. Sloping sides make the job slightly more difficult; therefore, it is better to cut out shapes already designed, cover them with transparent sheeting and then stick them in place on the shade with a heat-resistant glue. Alternatively the flowers may be arranged directly on to the lampshade and lacquered over with heat-resistant glue. Should the lampshade be other than cylindrical, you might find it difficult to cover the design with one piece of the adhesive sheeting, so in this case either cut out a circular or oval shape to cover each part of the design, or protect the flowers by covering them with a layer of nail lacquer.

Lampshades decorated thus are very attractive as the light enhances the colours and textures of the pressed materials. Do remember to choose your pressed flowers, etc., carefully, bearing in mind that they will be exposed to a great deal of light and a certain amount of heat. Dark brown autumn leaves make an excellent choice, together with flowers that have turned brown in the pressing book. Hydrangeas are first-class for this purpose.

Wastepaper bins may also be decorated using this method.

FRAMED PICTURE

In this last project you can use your imagination to the full as far as colour and design are concerned and select flowers, leaves, buds and grasses to make a really beautiful picture, which can be mounted and framed.

Choose your background material to complement the flowers you will use, be it card, velvet or silk. Place the dried specimens on it and move the pieces around until you are satisfied with the design; then glue each piece in place (remember, the smallest amount of glue). When you have completed your picture, cover it as soon as possible with a sheet of glass and either frame it yourself or have it done professionally, in which case it would be advisable to keep the glass and background together by means of cellotape around the edges, so as to ensure moisture will not get to the dried materials.

You will of course have thoughts of your own on which flowers and grasses to use, so experiment as you go to get the maximum out of the specimens that you have pressed. When using Honeysuckle, press all the florets and buds separately and reassemble them, using Senecio leaves instead of Honeysuckle leaves. Common Reed, Wood Melick, Wood Millet, Quaking Grass, Tufted Hair Grass, Rough Meadow Grass, Velvet Bent Grass, Buttercup, Cow

Parsley, and Daisy, if used on a green background, give a very pleasing effect and are ideal for the beginner as they have a beautiful natural flow. Buttercups add just a dash of brightness.

French Marigold, Japanese Maple, Russian Vine, Cow Parsley and Yarrow are also a lovely combination. The advantage of pressing French Marigolds is their immense variety of shades so that it is possible to compose a picture using very little foliage.

To compose a picture, using white on a green ground, the following may be used: African Anemone, Russian Vine (otherwise known as Bridal Veil), Orange Blossom, Hydrangea florets, Gypsophila, Seeded Globe Artichoke, young Yarrow leaves.

This is an example of how flowers that have turned white in the press may be used to give a pleasing effect on a dark background. Flowers that turn brown in the press look equally effective on darker brown backgrounds.

For a bouquet design, try Tufted Hair Grass, Mimosa, Delphiniums, Yellow Alyssum, green Hydrangea florets, Lobelia, Buttercups and the leaves of the Shrimp plant which vary in colour and size and therefore mingle well.

Flower-pressing is a 'gentle' art, which will give pleasure to both you and your friends, who will treasure your designs. The joy to be derived from the garden and countryside and the awareness of the great variety of plant life will inspire you to preserve our 'green and pleasant land' for future generations to enjoy and respect.

12 Puppets

MARLENE ENGLAND

PUPPETS! WHERE? Well, everywhere. Perhaps there is a country in the world that does not have some form of puppetry; if so, there is a large gap in their entertainment.

No matter how simple, or how complicated (even a paper bag with a face painted on it can achieve some sort of magic), once the curtain of the puppet theatre rises and the act begins, the enchantment takes over. Often the simple,

Figures 12.1 & 2

well known, well loved stories are the most successful, for the audience can anticipate and become part of the show.

Puppets can be constructed from almost anything, depending on the character and the amount of movement and manipulation required, and they range from simple finger-puppets made of felt (Fig. 12.1) to a fully articulated cast of an opera or Shakespearian play (Fig. 12.2). The main types of puppets are: shadow-puppets (Fig. 12.3), glove-puppets (Fig. 12.4), rod-puppets (Fig. 12.5) and string-puppets or marionettes (Fig. 12.6).

Before embarking on the making of your puppet, give careful thought to its use and its user, for a small child would soon become hopelessly entangled in the complicated strings of a marionette and, by the same token, an older child would soon become frustrated by the limitations of a finger- or glove-puppet.

Above
Figure 12.3
Left to right
Figures 12.4 & 5

Materials and equipment

awl	gloves
drill	socks
screwdriver	balls
scissors, paint and glue	yoghourt pots
tenon and hacksaw	wooden rods
craft knife	cotton-reels
screw-rings and hooks	beads
plastic wood	wire
self-hardening clay	paper fasteners
wood	string
paper	paints
card	glue
fabric	

Shadow-puppets

Shadow-puppets are perhaps the oldest known of all puppets. The Chinese have used shadows as entertainment for at least 2000 years. In fact, the first puppet-master is said to have been Yang Shih and he is credited with making the first puppets and performing with them at the court of the Chu emperor Mu Wang in 1000 B.C.

The Indonesians, Indians and Greeks have a great tradition in the shadow-theatre and the secret of their arts was closely guarded and passed down through families from generation to generation. All the Middle Eastern peoples had shadow-puppets but the style of the figures differed from country to

Above
Figure 12.6
Left to right
Figures 12.7–10

Javanese

Iraqui

Turkish

Egyptian

country (Fig. 12.7–10). Also the method of operating the puppets varied. All shadow theatres had a religious significance at their beginning.

This type of puppet is a flat figure which casts a shadow on to a screen. The Chinese used translucent figures which were beautifully coloured; the material was thin leather, oiled to become transparent, and the rods were of wire and bamboo (Fig. 12.11).

Figure 12.11

PUPPETS

The best material for the shadow-figure is stiff card which can be cut with sharp scissors or, better still, with a craft-knife. Because the puppet is two-dimensional, the shape of the figure can first be drawn on to paper as an outline, and then the number of joints decided upon. Only the minimum of joints needed should be used, as each joint requires a control wire or rod. Figure 12.12 shows the first outline drawing. The number of joints showing the overlap required to make the joint and also the position for the control rods are shown in Fig. 12.13. The next step is to cut out from paper the parts of the drawing, including extra parts for the joints (Fig. 12.14), and then draw around these paper patterns on to stiff card and cut them out. Assemble the puppet, with arms and legs on each side of the body. Make a hole with a large darning needle or an awl through the centre of the joint positions (see Fig. 12.14). Use brass paper-fasteners for the joint. Remember not to make the joints too stiff and to have the flat head of the fastener on the side of the puppet which will rest against the screen. Fine wire or string can be used for joints instead of paper-fasteners. (Put your puppet pattern into an envelope to keep for future use.)

The control wires or rods are made from steel wire; or from such items as umbrella ribs, bicycle spokes or thin wooden rods. To extend the length, the wire can be inserted into a length of wood. To attach the rods to the puppet,

Left to right
Figures 12.12–15

ear

ear
cut 2

position
for rods

front
leg

cut 2

back leg

cut 2

first make two small holes at the position marked on the pattern for the supports (see Fig. 12.14), then make a small tight loop at one end of the wire rod using long-nosed pliers. The rod can then be stitched into place (Fig. 12.15). When this is done the puppet is ready for action.

SCREEN

An essential requirement is a screen made of translucent material. White paper will do very well but will soon tear; much better is a sheet of cotton material stretched tightly on a frame and held in a rigid upright position (Fig. 12.16).

LIGHTING

Light must fall evenly on to the screen and only the shadow of the puppet should be cast on to the screen. There are two ways of achieving this; the light can be fixed behind and just below the screen, between it and the puppeteer, and the puppet held close to the screen, with the rods held horizontally and attached at right angles to the back. Alternatively, the light is behind and above the puppeteer, who holds the rods in a perpendicular position from below (Fig. 12.17 & 18). In the first method the rods will not show but in the second the rods will always cast shadows.

For lighting the screen, a flood-lamp will give a more even light than a spot-lamp, which quickly loses brightness away from the centre of focus. Also, it is preferable to use one source of light rather than two, because of the danger of doubling the shadow. The position of the light is very important and is best found by experiment. Perhaps the best position is above and behind the puppeteer, but high enough for there to be no chance of the shadow from the puppeteer's head or arms being shown on the screen. Strip lighting is very effective if the light is to be thrown up from below the screen. Coloured lights can also be used for special effects.

Left to right
Figures 12.16–18

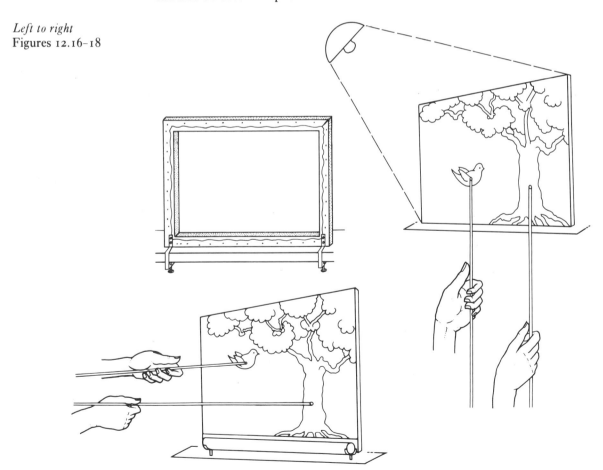

Left to right
Figures 12.19 & 20

SCENERY

The scenery can be made in many ways. A whole scene can be painted in coloured inks or water colour or in black and white paint on a single sheet of heavy translucent paper of the same size as the screen and then cut out. If the paper is thin it may wrinkle and fall away from the screen, so to prevent this a thin sheet of plastic can be fixed to the back of the scene; this will also give a smooth working-surface for the puppets. A groove running along the bottom ledge of the screen (Fig. 12.19) will help to support the scenery, which is just laid against the screen, and thus help to stop it being accidentally knocked over. Individual items of scenery, such as trees, buildings and furniture, by means of a length of stiff wire attached to the back, can be slotted into holes drilled in the floor of the stage along a line close to the screen (Fig. 12.20). Individual items can then be changed around. Transparent flimsy materials, lace, paper and card can be used effectively. The light will pass through them giving an illusion of distance. Painting the distant scenery, for example, mountains, with watered-down ink or water colour will also give this distant effect. Natural materials, such as grasses, twigs and seed-heads, make useful additions.

Glove- or hand-puppets

The most famous of traditional English puppets is of course Punch and Judy (Fig. 12.21). Excited and enthralled audiences of children can still be seen at the Punch and Judy shows, sadly few and far between now. Several European countries have their versions of Punch and Judy, always the same basic story and always glove-puppets. The heads and hands were usually carved from wood, the body being made of cloth to cover the puppeteer's hand and arm. He uses his first finger to hold and control the head movement, his thumb in one arm of the puppet and his second finger in the other arm (Fig. 12.22). This means the puppet can pick up and hold objects (Fig. 12.23) and put a lot of energy into its movements.

Left to right
Figures 12.21-23
Below
Figure 12.24

The heads of glove-puppets are usually large in proportion to hands and body, allowing exaggeration in the character. As most children enjoy acting, this easily controllable type of puppet is ideal for the beginner in the art of puppetry. The glove or body can be tailored to fit individual hands simply by drawing around the shape of the child's hand but allowing a good space for movement (Fig. 12.24). Being simple to make, a child can enjoy putting his or her own ideas into the design.

PUPPETS

A basic shape cut in felt, incorporating the head with the glove (Fig. 12.25) can then be turned into many characters or animals. Figure 12.26 shows an owl, decorated with various shades of brown felt, beads and paint. A very effective start perhaps to a play 'The Owl and the Pussycat' springs to mind!

Heads are usually made separately from the body and this gives greater articulation. A rubber ball is a good basis, or a modelled papier-maché head, but a piece of stocking or sock, stuffed, with the features made from felt and stuck on, will do very well (Fig. 12.27-29). A tube of cardboard or buckram then needs to be inserted into the head to form a neck, which also serves as the finger control (Fig. 12.30). Next, the body or glove is made from strong cotton material or felt. A completed clown is shown in Fig. 12.31, perhaps the start of a circus performance.

Left to right
Figures 12.25 & 26

Below
Figures 12.27–31

Fur fabric is useful and realistic, either for animals or as scraps used for hair, as on the clown. Wool, string, strips of paper or wood shavings (which make lovely curls) can be used too.

Sometimes legs are included on a glove-puppet. These are attached to the lower front edge of the glove and are not usually manipulated (Fig. 12.32). Large types of glove-puppets, such as crocodiles, frogs and snakes or birds, are operated by the use of the whole hand in the head of the puppet (Fig. 12.33). These usually have large open mouths or beaks and the operator's hand makes the movements.

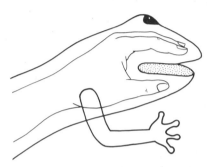 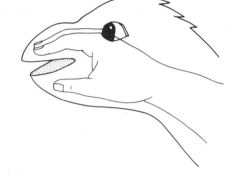

Left to right
Figures 12.32 & 33

Below
Figures 12.34–39

STAGE

Once you have made your puppet and decided to perform a play, then of course you will also need a stage. This can be a much simpler type of stage than is needed for a shadow play. In fact, the puppeteer can just stand behind a screen with a puppet on each hand (Fig. 12.34), although the puppets should not be far back from the front edge of the screen or the audience will not see them. The puppeteer can sit; this requires a lower screen with a curtain from above to hide him (Fig. 12.35). Arms soon tire holding up puppets, so a ledge to rest on, running along the top edge of the screen, is a great help (Fig. 12.36). A stage can quickly be improvised from a curtain stretched across an open doorway (Fig. 12.37) or from a table turned on its side (Fig. 12.38); rods supported by posts and draped with a curtain or an old sheet work well (Fig. 12.39). Providing the screen is large enough, more than one puppeteer can work at the same time.

Rod-puppets

Rod-puppets are similar in construction to glove-puppets and are held above a screen by the puppeteer, but, because they are controlled by rods, they can be made much larger. This type of puppet was known from early times in China, India and Africa, but Java has the greatest tradition of this type of puppetry. They were carved in wood, painted and dressed in decorative materials, sometimes silk with beads and sequins (Fig. 12.40).

PUPPETS

The greatest movement is in the head and arm action. The head is fixed to a long wooden rod, which goes right through the body, and this rod controls the movement of the head, which can be turned from side to side. Arms are jointed and are attached to the shoulders with string or cord; they are moved by thin rods attached to the hands (Fig. 12.41).

To manipulate the puppet, the puppeteer has to use both hands, one for the head and the other for the two arm control wires. If the puppet is large then weight can be a problem, so, if you can, dispense with the body completely. This is possible if the character has a gown or dress, if not, then a wooden shoulder-piece can be made, and a soft stuffed body can be attached to this, by means of glue or tacks. The lower part of the body is also glued to a wooden base (Fig. 12.42). Both the shoulder-piece and base must have holes drilled

Left to right
Figures 12.40–42

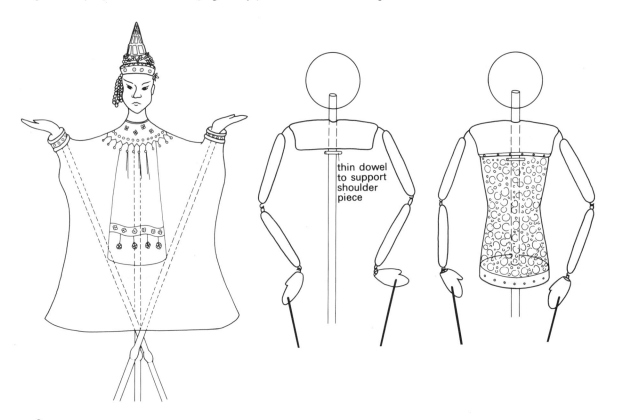

thin dowel
to support
shoulder
piece

through them to allow free movement of the central control rod. Heads and hands are usually carved from wood but can be made from felt or the new self-hardening modelling clay. Where the puppet has legs they are left to swing freely and not manipulated.

STAGE

The stage for the rod-puppets is similar to that of the glove-puppet, but a shelf would be a useful addition to help support the puppets during a performance.

String-puppets

PUPPETS

Left to right
Figures 12.43 & 44

This type of puppet is three-dimensional and has legs which can be operated; this gives more scope to the movements, such as dance routines or acrobatics.

The beginner should try a simple string-puppet with five strings only (Fig. 12.43) and, as more skill is achieved, more strings can be added, i.e. to back, elbows and feet. A five-string figure will have strings from head, hands and feet. Animals must not be forgotten; a wonderful caterpillar can be constructed from cotton-reels using four strings for manipulation (Fig. 12.44). All joints need spacers of some kind and wooden beads used between the cotton-reels are ideal and give free movement. Cotton-reels can also be used to make figures. Man-made sewing-thread is wound on to longer reels than the traditional cotton

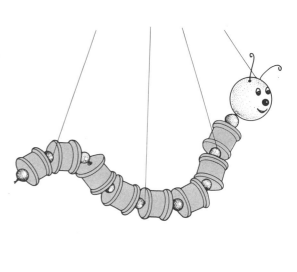

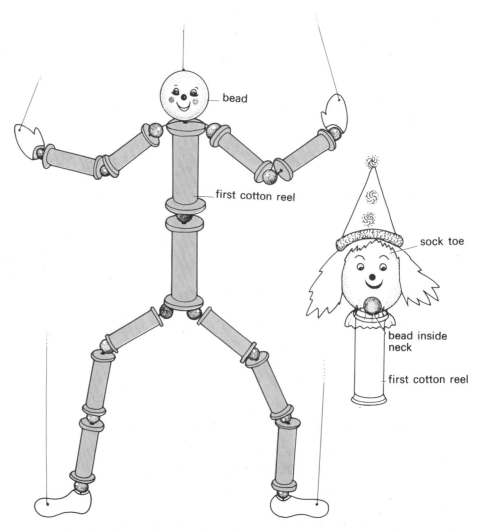

bead

first cotton reel

sock toe

bead inside
neck

first cotton reel

Left to right
Figures 12.45 & 46

and these are useful for the body of the puppet; there are also some very slim types of reel which can be used for arms and legs (Fig. 12.45). A soft head can be made from the toe end of a sock and stuffed with soft filling (Fig. 12.46); the hands and feet are made from felt. When felt is used for hands and feet, it is necessary to weight them; metal washers or dress-maker's weights will do.

Wood is the traditional material for string-puppets and has the advantage that it will take screw-rings, eyes and tacks, and can be drilled and carved. If you are not a wood-carver, then wooden balls sold in craft shops make good heads and features can be added on, using plastic wood.

If your puppet is to represent a human figure, study the movements of people around you; look at their shapes and proportions. Decide on the size of your puppet's head, then the body-length and length of arms and legs. If you want your puppet to have human proportions, then you will find there are approximately seven head-lengths in the height of an adult, but only five head-lengths in the height of a 4-year-old child. These proportions can of course be

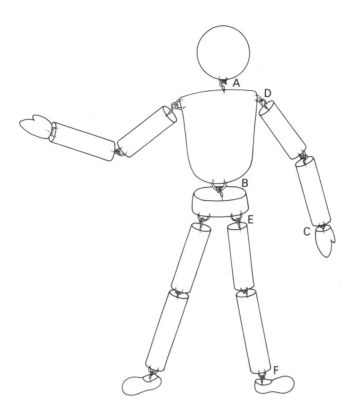

Figure 12.47

Figures 12.48 & 49

altered to exaggerate the character of the puppet; you may want a giant with a large head and hands, or a clown with extra large shoes.

The joints on the illustrated puppet (Fig. 12.47) are made by linking screw-rings and screw-hooks together: between the head and shoulder-piece (A), waist and hips (B), arms and hands (C), arms and shoulder (D), legs and hips (E) and legs and feet (F); as you make each joint, screw the hooks as far in as possible to close the gap. Features are then painted on to the head or built up from plastic wood (Fig. 12.48 & 49), hair is added, and wool or scraps of fur fabric can be glued into place. Then your puppet is ready for stringing. This puppet has five strings from head, hands and knees; this will allow head move-ment with a nodding action and free arm and leg movement. The hands, if made from wood, will need a small hole drilled through the centre of the back. When using self-hardening clay for hands, the hole can be made while the clay is still fairly soft.

Next a small screw-ring is placed in the top of the puppet's head. This will be hidden by hair or a hat and will take the head control string. A second string is passed through the back of the hand and knotted on the palm of the hand; this is a continuous running string (Fig. 12.50). The string for the legs is attached to the knee-joint and is also continuous.

These strings are then attached to a control bar and, as there are only five strings, the simplest is a horizontal cross-bar, sometimes called an aeroplane control. This is suitable for puppets up to 30 cm (12 in) in height. It consists

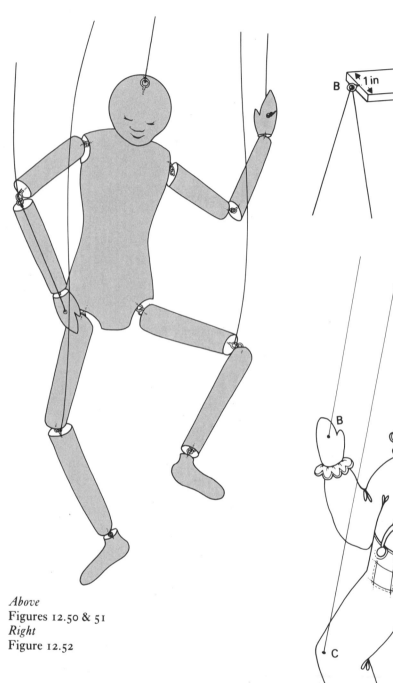

Above
Figures 12.50 & 51
Right
Figure 12.52

of two pieces of wood, each 15 cm (6 in) by 2.5 cm (1 in) by 1.75 cm ($\frac{1}{2}$ in). The cross-bar pivots on the hook so that it can be twisted to fold flat (Fig. 12.51). A large cup-hook is very useful and can also be used to hang up the puppet when not in use. Use strong twine, thin cord or string, or nylon cord for stringing.

The string for the head is usually fixed (Fig. 12.51) at (A), but those for the arms (B) and legs (C) are continuous, run-through strings. Here screw-hooks are used; this enables the operator to lift off strings should they become tangled. The screw-hook must be well screwed into the control-bar once the string is in position or it may slip off the hook when in use. If the strings do become tangled, releasing one string will often release the rest. Make sure the strings are long enough, when attached to the control bar, for the puppet to stand in a natural position.

CLOTHING

Clothing, of course, will depend on the character of your puppet, but the costume should be cut so as not to impede the movement of the joints. The type of material used is very important, thick heavy materials are not suitable and, unless there is a special need, stiff material should be avoided. The most suitable are soft cottons, jersey, silk and knitted material which will drape into small folds.

A scrap-box is a valuable asset so collect scraps of lace, edgings, ribbons, tassels, coloured embroidery cottons and beads. All will be needed at some time.

The clown in Fig. 12.52 has a baggy one-piece costume made from brightly coloured cotton material and decorated with pom-poms. The leg-string from the knee-joint is pushed through the costume with the aid of a darning-needle.

There are so many types of clowns, from the white-faced clown, a very serious character with spangled costume, to the red-nosed, baggy-trousered, big-footed, knock-about clowns (Fig. 12.53), that a whole performance could be given over to their antics. Perhaps a small bucket filled with confetti could be picked up and tipped by your puppet clown. Practice will soon make perfect. It will help to practice in front of a long mirror, as it is quite difficult to judge the movements from above.

STAGE

Shadow-, glove- and rod-puppets are all operated from below stage but the string-puppet is operated from above (Fig. 12.54).

If a stage is being used (Fig. 12.55), the puppeteer will need a platform or bench to stand on but string-puppets can be worked without a stage (Fig. 12.56). The puppeteer can simply be dressed in black, the light dimmed, and a spotlight shone on to the performing puppets; or the puppeteer can work behind a waist-high screen or curtain (Fig. 12.57). The interest of the audience is soon focused on the puppets and the operator forgotten.

Right
Figure 12.53
Below
Figure 12.54

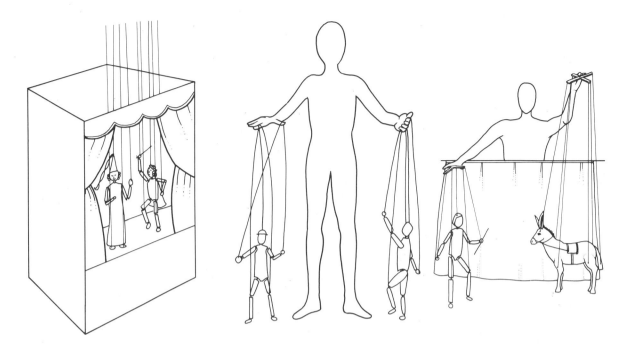

Left to right
Figures 12.55–57

Below
Figures 12.58 & 59

Although string-puppets are more difficult to make and manipulate than glove- or rod-puppets, they do give the illusion of moving freely. The control depends on the balance between the action of the puppeteer and the weight of the puppet. Feet and hands should be made of heavy material; wood is most suitable. Every puppet must be planned for its particular character and so the story or play should be worked out first. Also the size of the puppets must be decided upon. Their size determines the size of the stage and scenery.

Projects

SIMPLE GLOVE-PUPPET

You will require: one glove, one rubber ball, scissors, paint and glue.

Cut off the first and third finger of the glove, turn in the remaining edges and stitch across to neaten (Fig. 12.58). Cut a hole large enough for your first finger in the rubber ball. Paint a face on it and glue on hair using rubber cement (Fig. 12.59 & 60). Hair can be made from wool, string or fur fabric.

If you have used a left glove, you will operate this puppet with your right hand by tucking down your 3rd and 4th finger (Fig. 12.61) putting your right thumb into the left glove thumb, your right first finger into the middle finger of the glove, and your right middle finger into the little finger of the glove. Now push your first finger into the rubber ball and you have your puppet (Fig. 12.62).

SIMPLE ROD-PUPPET: A WIZARD

You will require: one yoghourt tub, a ping-pong ball, a length of dowel, cardboard, glue, trimmings, needle and thread.

Left to right
Figures 12.60 & 61
Below
Figure 12.62

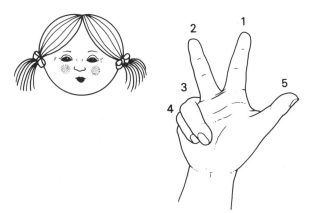

Using a paper pattern made from the diagram (Fig. 12.63), cut out the body from brightly coloured cotton material. Stitch the side seams, leaving the neck and lower edge open.

Make a hole in the ping-pong ball large enough to insert the dowel rod. This can be done by heating a metal knitting needle or an awl in a flame, then piercing the ping-pong ball. A hole is made in the base of the yoghourt tub in the same way. Glue the dowel into the ping-pong ball, using contact glue. Next push the dowel rod through the neck of the dress and through the hole in the tub. Secure the neck of the dress with a dab of glue to the rod just below the ping-pong ball head. Then, with the dress over the tub, glue the lower edge of the dress to the wide edge of the tub (Fig. 12.64).

The hat is made from a cardboard cone, painted and decorated with stars and spangles (Fig. 12.65). The hair and beard are of wool or stranded cotton, glued into place. Paint the features, acrylic paint is best. Then glue the hat on to his head and your rod-puppet is finished (Fig. 12.66).

Left to right
Figures 12.63–66

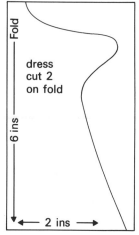

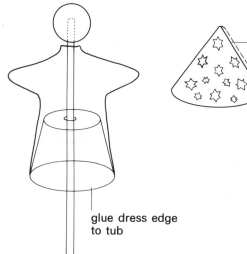

glue dress edge
to tub

POP-UP PUPPET

You will require: a yoghourt tub, dowel rod, ping-pong ball, cotton material, needle and thread and glue.

The process is the same as for the rod-puppet but this time the puppet will pop out of the yoghourt tub. Cut out the dress using the diagram (Fig. 12.67), then glue the lower edge to the inner edge of the tub (Fig. 12.68).

A hat is cut from a cardboard circle (Fig. 12.69) to fit around the ping-pong ball, painted and trimmed with scraps of lace, flowers and small feathers.

When the rod is pulled down the puppet disappears into the tub (Fig. 12.70), so use soft material for the dress otherwise the tub will not contain the whole of the puppet.

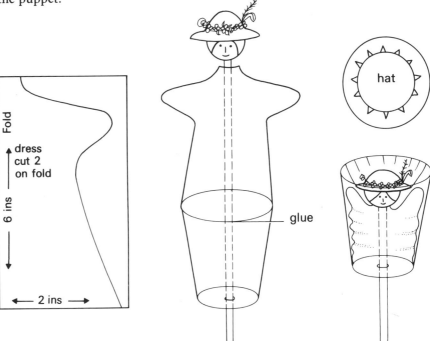

Left to right
Figures 12.67–70

Index

Numbers in **bold** refer to colour plates. Those in *italic* refer to the page numbers of figures. Other numbers refer to text pages.

ACKNOWLEDGEMENTS
*Grateful acknowledgement is made by the editor and publisher to Gillian M. Griffin, who provided illustrations for colour plates
10 and 12, and to Robin Fletcher who provided illustrations for the remaining colour plates.*